D0789989

The Virtuous Life

OF A CHRIST-CENTERED WIFE

The Virtuous Life

OF A CHRIST-CENTERED WIFE

18 Powerful Lessons for Personal Growth

New York Times Best-Selling Author
DARLENE SCHACHT

The Ministry of
Time-Warp Wife

All Scripture unless otherwise noted is taken from The KJV Bible

The Virtuous Life of a Christ-Centered Wife:
18 Powerful Lessons for Personal Growth
ISBN 978-0-9780262-3-3
Time-Warp Wife
Suite 5-1377 Border Street
Winnipeg, Manitoba
R3H ON1

Copyright © 2014 by Darlene Schacht

Cover design by Darlene Schacht
Image from Bigstock.com

ALL RIGHTS RESERVED
No part of this book may be reproduced in any form—photocopying,
electronic, audio recording, or otherwise—without written permission
from the author.

Find Darlene Schacht on the web here:
Blog: TimeWarpWife.com
Facebook: timewarpwife
Twitter: timewarpwife
Pinterest: timewarpwife

If you enjoy this book, please leave a review at Amazon.

*This book is dedicated to my daughter Madison,
an incredible young woman who is growing in virtue
right before my eyes.*

CONTENTS

Preface   *ix*

Introduction   *xiii*

LESSON ONE
What is Virtue?   *1*

LESSON TWO
A Kind Wife   *9*

LESSON THREE
A Diligent Wife   *19*

LESSON FOUR
A Self-Controlled Wife   *27*

LESSON FIVE
A Trustworthy Wife   *37*

LESSON SIX
An Encouraging Wife   *41*

LESSON SEVEN
A Pure Wife   *47*

LESSON EIGHT
A Loving Wife   *57*

LESSON NINE
A Patient Wife   *63*

LESSON TEN
A Humble Wife   *73*

LESSON ELEVEN
A Faithful Wife 79

LESSON TWELVE
A Forgiving Wife 89

LESSON THIRTEEN
A Joyful Wife 95

LESSON FOURTEEN
A Passionate Wife 101

LESSON FIFTEEN
A Radiant Wife 105

LESSON SIXTEEN
A Balanced Wife 111

LESSON SEVENTEEN
A Good Wife 117

LESSON EIGHTEEN
A Courageous Wife 123

About the Author 129

PREFACE

THE VIRTUOUS LIFE OF A CHRIST-CENTERED WIFE is written in the format of an 18-part study for daily or weekly reflection. Not only is it a powerful tool for personal growth, it's also an ideal study-guide for small groups.

Each lesson leads you through one virtue at a time, offering you applicable and inspiring ways to grow closer to God and your husband.

Every lesson concludes with the S-O-A-P method of study, prompting you to dig deeper as follows:

S   **Scripture:** You'll be provided with a portion of Scripture to meditate on.

O   **Observation:** This is a good chance to journal your thoughts. What are some personal observations?

   If you're in a group study this might include some things you'd like to share with the others.

A   **Application:** How can you apply this to your life? Are there changes you'd like to make? Is God prompting you to focus on something?

P   **Prayer:** Each lesson includes a short prayer in hopes that you will invite God to play a vital role in this personal journey.

I'd rather be a crown than a trophy wife;
I'd rather have virtue than vogue.

INTRODUCTION

The three hardest tasks in the world are neither physical feats nor intellectual achievements, but moral acts: to return love for hate, to include the excluded, and to say, "I was wrong."

SYDNEY J. HARRIS

SOME DAYS I LOOK AROUND AND can't help but think that I don't measure up. Don't we all? I'm not a hockey mom, a trophy wife, Martha Stewart, or Beth Moore. I'm just me. I don't run marathons, knit hats, bake well, or scrapbook. I read.

Barely five feet tall, I look up to other women in more ways than one. I still have this feeling that if they divided the women in my neighborhood into two teams I'd be the last one picked. I'm not the life of the party. I'm the introvert that struggles to socialize while others throw their heads back in laughter and chit-chat with ease.

I'm a star at Pinterest fails. I have one crooked arm. And I wake up with the wildest hair that needs to be tamed.

Insecurity—it's a lie that Satan wants us to believe. We aren't perfect and he's sure to point that out to us every single day. He'll never show us our importance because in doing so we wouldn't realize how important we are to God.

If we hope to live in victory, we must keep our eyes off of the world and on the One who perfects us through grace.

Moses didn't think he could be used by God because he wasn't eloquent enough. And when God called Gideon to save Israel from the Midianites his reply was,

> *"Oh my Lord, wherewith shall I save Israel? Behold, my family is poor in Manasseh, and I am the least in my father's house."*
>
> JUDGES 6:15

How many times are we held back because we're not good enough either? How many days are we discouraged because we don't realize the extent of God's grace?

I'm not a perfect wife, but I cling to the verse in Proverbs 12:4, *"A virtuous woman is a crown to her husband."*

With joy I'm reminded that I'd rather be a crown than a trophy wife, and that I'd rather have virtue than vogue.

Who can find a virtuous woman? For her price is far above rubies. – Proverbs 31:10

You're so much more than just another pretty face; you're deeply loved by a God Who numbers your hair. The same God who painted spots on ladybugs' backs, and lights up our skies with fireflies created you, redeemed you, and knows you by name.

Have you surrendered your life to the Lord? Here's merely a glimpse of who we become through His grace:

A friend:

> *Henceforth I call you not servants; for the servant knoweth not what his lord doeth: but I have called you friends; for all things that I have heard of my Father I have made known unto you.*
>
> JOHN 15:15

His children:

But as many as received him, to them gave He power to become the sons of God, even to them that believe on his name.

JOHN 1:12

Joint heirs with Christ:

And if children, then heirs; heirs of God, and joint-heirs with Christ; if so be that we suffer with him, that we may be also glorified together.

ROMANS 8:17

Free:

Stand fast therefore in the liberty wherewith Christ hath made us free, and be not entangled again with the yoke of bondage.

GALATIANS 5:1

Redeemed:

In whom we have redemption through his blood, the forgiveness of sins, according to the riches of his grace;

EPHESIANS 1:7

A New Creation:

> *So then, if anyone is in Christ, he is a new creation;*
> *what is old has passed away–look, what is new has come.*
>
> 2 CORINTHIANS 5:17

Seated with Christ:

> *[He] hath raised us up together, and made us sit together*
> *in heavenly places in Christ Jesus:*
>
> EPHESIANS 2:6

And the list goes on...

Seriously–does any of this compare to a bad day, or what people might think about you?

Do people point out your flaws, your mistakes, or your past?

Who you *were* can never compare to who you *are* in Christ.

You were bought, you were purchased, you were redeemed, you were set free, and you–yes YOU are loved by an almighty God!

LESSON ONE

WHAT IS VIRTUE?

Our virtues are like crystals hidden in rocks.
No man shall find them by any soft ways, but by
the hammer and by fire.

HENRY WARD BEECHER

MY DAUGHTER STARTED RUNNING LAST YEAR. Three minutes walking/two minutes running during the first week, two minutes of each during the second week, and so on...

She wasn't a happy runner. In fact, she hated the idea at first. But during that first week I told her that I was certain of one thing–after a while she'd not only enjoy her workouts, she'd look forward to them.

Fast forward a month and I had a runner in the house. Last night she bought workout clothes and today she told me that she doesn't like the idea of missing a day. If she could be on the treadmill 24/7 she would.

Isn't it funny how our body reacts to exercise?

In much the same way, so does our flesh. It's not always easy to control our temper, hold our tongue, or exercise patience, but the more that we exercise those muscles, the easier it gets.

This morning I woke up with three things on my mind: conforming, transforming, and virtue. No sooner did I open my eyes and I was reaching for a pen.

What is it, Lord? I asked... *How do these all fit together, and what is Your message for me?*

As the day went on, my thoughts turned to His Word.

Looking to the Bible we see two women referred to as "virtuous": one is Ruth and the other is the Proverbs 31 woman. Certainly there are many other women in the Bible who lived a virtuous life, but these two are interesting because they show a spectrum of virtue in action that encompasses both the big and the small.

Ruth sacrificed much when she gave up her people to follow Naomi, and the Proverbs 31 woman made sacrificial choices throughout the day as she conformed to those things that were good.

I like Matthew Henry's wise commentary on the word "virtue," found in Proverbs 31: *A virtuous woman—a woman of strength (so the word is), though the weaker vessel, yet made strong by wisdom and grace, and the fear of God: it is the same word that is used in the character of good judges (Ex. 18:21), that they are able men, men qualified for the business to which they are called, men of truth, fearing God. So it follows, A virtuous woman is a woman of spirit, who has the command of her own spirit and knows how to manage other people's, one that is pious and industrious, and a help meet for a man... A virtuous woman is a woman of resolution, who, having espoused good principles, is firm and steady to them, and will not be frightened with winds and clouds from any part of her duty.*

We see here that a virtuous woman *conforms* to her principles.

When I conform my will, my desires, and my passions for the good of my family I conform myself to the will of God.

I carefully choose the word "good" here because there's a difference between being a doormat and conforming to a life that draws your family closer to the Lord and strengthens your marriage.

Virtue is all about our behavior. It's an act of yielding our lives to our principles, which is not always easy, but always rewarding.

There's a will to do good in every one of us, but whether or not we choose to exercise and develop that goodness determines our character.

> *And beside this, giving all diligence, add to your faith virtue; and to virtue knowledge; And to knowledge temperance; and to temperance patience; and to patience godliness; And to godliness brotherly kindness; and to brotherly kindness charity. For if these things be in you, and abound, they make you that ye shall neither be barren nor unfruitful in the knowledge of our Lord Jesus Christ.*
>
> 2 PETER 1:5-8

We all battle against the flesh in one way or another. If you're yelling at your kids, fighting with your husband, overeating, or abusing internet time you might be feeling discouraged. The thing is that we're given a choice to either continue down the path we're going or to make changes that develop stronger character and a happier life.

Why Is Virtue Important?

First and foremost we're saved by grace. There's nothing that we can do to earn our salvation. Salvation has been imputed to us by God through faith in His Son, Jesus Christ. The thing is however, those who believe in Jesus, believe He is Lord. Lord of the universe and Lord of their lives.

His wisdom exceeds ours, when it's both comfortable and uncomfortable; on the good days and bad. Those who love God are willing to give up every selfish ambition and every sinful desire to follow His will.

This doesn't mean that we walk *perfectly* by any means. That's where the grace of God is vital to our faith.

It's by the grace of God that we're saved through faith in Jesus Christ. So while I'm not perfect, I can rest in the knowledge that my Redeemer is!

We all struggle in this world. We all have good intentions, but our flesh keeps pulling us back.

Have you ever made a decision to do something worthwhile? Maybe you wanted to change a bad habit or incorporate a new one. A few days in, you gave up. Even though you knew that this was a good decision for you, you messed up (again) and you're down on yourself because you're weak.

It's called being human. Our flesh is constantly at war with our Spirit and there's a battle to be won.

The important thing is that every time we fall, we have the opportunity to get back up again and get back in the race.

Leave the sin of the past behind you and focus on the road ahead. And if you should fall? Pick yourself up and get back in the race.

We're growing in grace. Learning what areas of our lives God is calling us to, and how to best set our sail.

2 Peter chapter 1 is key to this study. Here we see that we're called to glory *and* virtue:

3 According as his divine power hath given unto us all things that pertain unto life and godliness, through the knowledge of him that hath called us to glory and virtue: 4 Whereby are given unto us exceeding great and precious promises: that by these ye might be partakers of the divine nature, having escaped the corruption that is in the world through lust. 5 And beside this, giving all diligence, add to your faith virtue; and to virtue knowledge; 6 And to knowledge temperance; and to temperance patience; and to patience godliness; 7 And to godliness brotherly kindness; and to brotherly kindness charity. 8 For if these things be in you, and abound, they make you that ye shall neither be barren nor unfruitful in the knowledge of our Lord Jesus Christ.

2 PETER 1:3-8

And so we see that virtue is something we build on the foundation of our faith. It's about being concerned about right and wrong as we seek to serve God.

Faith is the driving force behind virtue. Faith powers our decision to change; virtue is the modification of our behavior, as we conform our lives to our principles.

Virtue Takes Effort, Values Don't

Values are things that we deem as important. Virtues are characteristics of a person that come about by the way that we live. If we want to be patient, we must *exercise* patience. If we want to be self-controlled, we must *exercise* self-control. And if we want to be kind, then we *must show kindness to others.*

The reason that we walk in virtue isn't to earn ourselves brownie points, or to proclaim our goodness to the world. C.S. Lewis wrote, *"Don't shine so others can see you. Shine so that through you, others can see Him."*

Aspiring to be seen is in direct contrast to virtue which stems from a heart of humility.

It's the Holy Spirit that convicts us, and God that carries us through. Without Him we wouldn't have any peace, we wouldn't have hope, and we wouldn't have joy. These are merely a few of the ways He equips us for the journey.

> *For it is God which worketh in you both to will and to do of his good pleasure.*
>
> PHILIPPIANS 2:13

Finally, how is virtue different than the fruit of the Spirit? In many ways they are similar because they are both characteristics of a Christ-centered life, but they differ in that virtue is the act of conforming and the fruit is the result of one whose life is conformed to Christ.

Chapter by chapter, we'll go through the virtues. Not every virtue, as I could write on this topic forever. (I've seen some lists with only a handful of virtues and others with over 600!)

This book will focus on the most common virtues and the ones that best pertain to marriage:

- Purity
- Self-control
- Love
- Diligence
- Patience
- Kindness
- Humility
- Faith
- Forgiveness
- Joy
- Passion

- Radiance
- Encouragement
- Balance
- Goodness
- Trustworthy
- Courage

Virtue calls us to action. As we exercise each one of these, they bring our flesh in line with our Spirit.

It's one thing to know what's good, and it's another to walk in obedience to the knowledge that we have received. Not always easy, but obedience to our faith is always worth the effort it takes!

S-O-A-P

Scripture

Read Proverbs 31:10-31

Observation

What are some of your personal observations from this lesson?

Application

How can you apply this to your life?

Prayer

Dear Heavenly Father,

I pray that you will guide me in virtue. Teach me to yield my flesh to the Spirit, to listen to Your voice, and to obey Your commands.

Help me to grow in my role as a wife. And may I learn to love as You love, and to freely give as You give. Amen.

LESSON TWO

A KIND WIFE

*The smallest act of kindness is worth more than
the grandest intention.*

OSCAR WILDE

MICHAEL DESERVES MORE THAN LEFTOVERS.

Leftover food? That's okay; especially when I've made
something good like lasagna, beef stir-fry, or chili. Then I'll
have him calling me the next day to ensure there's enough left
over for dinner. In fact, a lot of the things I make taste even
better the second day than they did the first time around.

What I'm talking about in this chapter however isn't a
matter of what's left in the refrigerator at the end of the day; it's
about what's left of *me*.

After a long day, do I offer him leftovers, or do I put in the
effort to be his companion and friend?

*And be ye kind one to another, tenderhearted, forgiving
one another, even as God for Christ's sake hath forgiven
you.*

EPHESIANS 4:32

Most relationships start out as friendships. We're gentle, kind, compassionate, and determined to win his heart. In a good marriage friendship doesn't end and you never stop pursuing his heart.

But the fact is that life is busy. We're driving kids to play dates, taking puppies to the vet, cooking dinner, making lunches, helping at the church, grocery shopping, caring for sick ones, bathing children, getting gas, cleaning house, doing laundry, planting flowers, pulling weeds, and the list goes on…

Who has the time or effort at the end of the day to keep giving?

The answer is found in the following parable, I think it's one of the best examples of kindness found in scripture.

Luke chapter ten tells us how a man was traveling from Jerusalem to Jericho when he fell among thieves. They robbed him, wounded him, and left him half dead.

A priest came by and passed on the other side. Then a Levite came by, looked at him and passed on the other side too.

Finally a Samaritan came by who had compassion on him. He went out of his way to ensure this man's safety taking him to an inn where he stayed with him until morning.

Before leaving he gave the innkeeper two pence and promised to reimburse any extra expenses the man might incur.

What stands out to me the most in this story is that kindness goes out of its way. It doesn't wait for an opportune time to give, but is ready and willing to drop what it's doing to mend the heart of another.

The Good Samaritan offered more than his leftovers, and he offered more than a half-hearted attempt at mercy and kindness.

What does Jesus say about that? "Go and do likewise."

Kindness can be found in those moments when we pause long enough to reach out and show someone we care. Offer a smile, a phone call, or kind word of encouragement.

Pick up on his love language and start practicing it. Little seeds grow in abundance when they stem from the heart.

But, you might say, *my husband doesn't deserve it.* And that could very well be true. It's not easy to be kind to someone who isn't kind in return, so why bother?

The answer to that is shown in the character of Our Heavenly Father. In Romans 2 we're shown that the intent of God's kindness is *to lead us to repentance,* therefore it makes little sense to withhold kindness from those who deserve it the least.

> *Do you show contempt for the riches of his kindness, forbearance and patience, not realizing that God's kindness is intended to lead you to repentance?*
>
> ROMANS 2:4

It might not be easy–virtue rarely is–but it builds character in those who are exercised by it.

Most importantly an unselfish act of kindness is a beautiful way to bring glory to God!

> *She openeth her mouth with wisdom; and in her tongue is the law of kindness.*
>
> PROVERBS 31:26

Put on Kindness

After 25 years I've gotten used to Michael's body language.

I can tell when this man is in a great mood, and I can also tell when something heavy is on his mind. I know when he's happy, and I know when he's mad. He doesn't have to say a word for me to read him. In fact he doesn't even have to turn and face me. I sense the mood.

It was everything, from the way he carried his body, to the swiftness of each step that moved me to ask him, "Is something wrong, Michael?"

"You even have to ask?!" he snapped back at me. "After the way you spoke to me earlier, you shouldn't be surprised at all that I'm angry."

I sat there for a minute thinking about a conversation we had just an hour before. It wasn't that I was rude—at least I didn't *think* so. I had simply expressed the fact that I was disappointed.

We had just come back from a gathering during which time we barely spoke two words to each other. Pulled in two different directions he spent time with the guys and I with the girls. I understand this will happen. And I certainly don't expect Michael to walk a three-legged-race with me, but barely two words? When I go out with my husband, I want to spend *some* time with him.

Here's the thing. We're two different people who communicate in two different ways. And I will admit that my "expression" can be a little negative at times. It's one thing to communicate, and it's another to nag which is something I'm still working on.

"Mom," Madison looked over at me, "Aren't you going to go say something to him?"

In other words, my daughter was pointing out the fact that it was time for me to put on a cloak of kindness. Smart girl.

Kindness is a virtue. It doesn't come easy to us unless we exercise that area of our life. It's more than simply a *desire* to do good to others, *it's the behavior itself.*

Kindness doesn't sit around analyzing a situation to determine whether this person is right or that person is wrong. Kindness is a charitable gift–it reaches out to those in need.

Whether it's easy or not, we are commanded in scripture to put on kindness. We're commanded to be compassionate people because that's Who our Savior is.

It's all about looking up. Looking to *Christ* for our example and looking to Him for our reward.

Initiation is the core of kindness. Jesus reached out to this world while we were in darkness and sin. He didn't sit around waiting for mankind to be perfect–He made the first move.

As difficult as it might be at times, we have the ability to choose our attitude at any time for the good. When someone gets under our skin, we can be impatient and vindictive or we can exercise the virtue of kindness.

It's especially important to remember this when we don't *feel* like it because that's when it becomes sacrifice.

> *Put on then, as God's chosen ones, holy and beloved, compassionate hearts, kindness, humility, meekness, and patience.*
>
> Colossians 3:12, ESV

There have been times when I sense that I'm a little angry or grumpy, and even though I know that I can let go of it and smile, I choose to hang on to it.

Praise God for His grace as He gently leads this work in progress.

I'm always encouraging wives to joyfully serve the Lord and their families. And the reason I choose this focus is because I firmly believe that in many cases our attitude can set the tempo in our home.

Have you ever heard the saying, "When mama's happy, everyone's happy?" I know it to be true in our home because a good attitude is not only contagious it offers a sense of assurance to others. It sends out an empowering message of contentment which is one that I want my kids to pick up on.

What I also want my kids to see is kindness in action. Not just kindness that comes *easy*, but *kindness to those who don't always deserve it.*

I had one of those proud-mommy-moments last night when I asked Madison, "If you were praying for a boyfriend. What five qualities would you ask God to include?"

Her answer was beautiful, and unlike most teenagers who might have put "a hot guy" at the top of their list:

1. *Christian*
2. *Generous*
3. *Someone who is kind to those who are not the nicest of people.*
4. *A MUSIC LOVER*
5. *.... I'll think about it*

Number five turned out to be "someone who has a great sense of humor," but did you happen to catch number three? She gets it!

Being kind to people who are nice to us is nothing more than an exchange of emotions. But real character is found in those who freely give without keeping score.

> *But I say unto you, Love your enemies, bless them that curse you, do good to them that hate you, and pray for them which despitefully use you, and persecute you;*
>
> MATTHEW 5:44

Marriage isn't about *you* and it isn't about *me*. It's about *centering our relationship on Jesus Christ* who freely gave of Himself when we least deserved it. God is kind to both the *just* and to the *unjust*.

> *That ye may be the children of your Father which is in heaven: for he maketh his sun to rise on the evil and on the good, and sendeth rain on the just and on the unjust.*
>
> MATTHEW 5:45

It only makes sense when we take the focus off of ourselves and turn them onto our Lord.

When I think of a kind wife, these are 7 of the habits that stand out to me most:

1   **She's affectionate** – All human beings benefit from affection. A smile, a kiss, a warm embrace when you walk in through door... These are the things that remind us we're loved.

2   **She's understanding** - Although we don't always agree with one another, it's a blessing when someone makes an effort to understand our point of view, isn't it? It takes an open heart and a listening ear.

3   **She looks to God to sharpen her character** - When we pattern our lives after our Savior, we surrender our lives to His will. Regardless of what pop-culture is doing, our decisions are based on truth.

4   **She's strengthened by prayer** - Prayer is an important step in reshaping our lives. If we want to center our marriage around Christ, first and foremost, we need to surrender our heart to His will.

5 **She knows that a kind word turns away wrath** - We all know this, but do we practice it enough? Kind words are powerful. They can diffuse a situation and calm a troubled heart.

6 **She builds up her husband instead of tearing him down** - Listening to him, making an effort to be cheerful, and ignoring his faults are just a few of the ways we can build up our husbands in a world that is tearing them down.

7 **She's not perfect, but she's growing in grace** - There are those who see virtue as impossibility. *"We all can't be this perfect, and we all can't be this strong."*

While that is true, it's important to remember that building virtue on faith is a life-long journey upon which the road is paved by His grace.

Just so you know, I did put on a cloak of kindness, and I did go down to the man cave to see Michael. And just so you know... one kiss on the forehead had him asking, "So what do you want to do today, honey?"

S-O-A-P

Scripture

Read Luke 10:25-37

Observation

What are some of your personal observations from this lesson?

Application

How can you apply this to your life?

Prayer

Dear Heavenly Father,

Please teach me to be affectionate and understanding toward others. I pray that my words will be used to edify and build up those around me.

Grant me the strength to put on kindness when I least feel like it. Thank you for your grace as I'm growing in this area of my life. Amen.

LESSON THREE

A DILIGENT WIFE

*Great things are done by a series of small
things brought together.*

VINCENT VAN GOUGH

THE TOPIC OF DILIGENCE BRINGS UP the idea of hard work. And yeah, much of life can be hard work, and truly some things *should* be difficult, since we grow from experience and mature through each trial we face.

That's why diligence is a virtue, because through it we develop character.

How strong would we be if life was a downhill ride on a smooth slope? We wouldn't be as mature as we are nor would we be as compassionate. I doubt that we'd value the things that we have as much as do when we work for them.

Life's tough and let's face it, an uphill battle is never pleasant.

But here's the thing, anyone who's ever reached the top will tell you that the view is incomparable. They'll encourage you to keep on keeping on when the going gets tough.

There's beauty to be found in the life of a persistent and diligent wife. Countless couples will tell you that the hard work they put into their marriage over the years has been worth it.

Countless couples will tell you how happy they are after 25, 40, and 60 years!

If you're in a bad place, I'm not telling you this to discourage you or remind you of what you *don't* have. My hope is to encourage you to hold on with a fierce grip. We all have bad days. Some couples might have had bad weeks or bad years— I've been there--but I have to tell you that persistence pays off.

Regardless of where you are in your marriage you have the ability to love him so stubbornly that Christ can't be denied.

If you're facing an uphill battle, if you're going through trials, if you've hit a rough patch in your marriage get a fierce grip on his heart and refuse to let go.

If you want to see change, give love a constant and earnest effort seasoned with prayer.

> *And beside this, giving all diligence, add to your faith virtue; and to virtue knowledge;*
>
> 2 PETER 1:5

Looking to this verse in its original context, we see the word 'diligence' translated from the Greek word spoudē which is *an earnestness in accomplishing, promoting, or striving after anything.*

Perhaps a modern translation of the word diligence might further add to its clarity: *constant and earnest effort to accomplish what is undertaken.* (Dictionary.com)

When I think of the word diligence, I can't help but think of Paul's letter to the Philippians in chapter 3. He's a runner in a spiritual race, leaving anything behind that might weigh him down. He gave all diligence to the race before him and threw aside anything that stood in the way.

I'm reminded of a pair of running shoes I picked up a couple of years ago. You can barely feel the weight of one in the palm of your hand, but less weight equals faster feet, which is important in the long run. In fact many experienced runners believe that even a few ounces can make a difference in their overall time.

The virtue of diligence is *faith-focused determination*. It's the effort we put into nurturing our families because we know this brings glory to Him. It's the attention we give to our marriage as we bring ourselves into submission to His will. It's turning our back on sin and our eyes upon Jesus. Everything we do is pointing to one thing–His will for our lives.

Paul says, "This one thing I do…"

> *This one thing I do, forgetting those things which are behind, and reaching forth unto those things which are before, I press toward the mark for the prize of the high calling of God in Christ Jesus.*
>
> PHILIPPIANS 3:13-14

Stop and consider the race for a minute. What's weighing you down? Are you over-committed? Are you carrying around resentment, bitterness, anger or pride? Have you lost focus of what's *really* important? Is idleness consuming your time?

In Acts chapter 27 we read an interesting story about the apostle Paul and several other prisoners who were sailing to Italy under the supervision of Julias the centurion.

After making a stop and transferring ships, the winds were so rough that it was impossible to stay on course. They docked at the Island of Crete. By this time the stormy autumn weather made it impossible to continue on. Paul warned them that they should stay put, but they ignored him and continued the journey en route to a better harbor.

Here's where the life lesson comes in. While out at sea, they lost control, and in order to survive, *they had to lighten the ship.* On the first day they threw out the anchors, on the second day the cargo, and on the third day they threw out their tackle and provisions.

> *And when neither sun nor stars in many days appeared, and no small tempest lay on us, all hope that we should be saved was then taken away.*
>
> ACTS 27:20

It wasn't until they were fully reliant on God that they found a glimpse of hope. Hope was there all along, but sometimes we need to come to the end of our rope before we realize that we're resting in the palm of God's hand.

Paul advised them that God would rescue them, but that they must remain together.

In a final act of faith, they lightened the ship yet again and threw their food into the sea.

The ship and everything in it was destroyed, but every one of those men made it safely to shore.

Compare this:

> *Wherefore seeing we also are compassed about with so great a cloud of witnesses, let us lay aside every weight, and the sin which doth so easily beset us, and let us run with patience the race that is set before us, looking unto Jesus the author and finisher of our faith; who for the joy that was set before him endured the cross, despising the shame, and is set down at the right hand of the throne of God.*
>
> HEBREWS 12:1-3

A couple sets out to make their marriage work. That's the intention of every loving young couple. But somehow sin makes its way through the door. It distracts you, it deceives you, and it entices you into tearing each other down.

Like fierce wind on a mighty sea, sin makes it impossible to stay the course until you're willing to lighten the ship. Throw off everything that is weighing you down, and grab hold of the Savior. He'll bring you safely to shore.

Another thing that's important to diligence is focus.

A marriage is two people on a life-long mission. Whether we notice it or not we all go into marriage with a goal or two in mind. And whatever that goal or mission is, will be different for every couple.

The key is to have the same goal as your husband, and the *master* key is to have a goal that's focused on the Lord.

A few years ago, when I was setting up a website, a friend asked me what my "mission statement" was.

"My mission?" I asked him, "Why do I need a mission?"

I should probably mention that this guy was a branding expert. He worked with some of the biggest companies out there formulating mission statements, but even so he knew that a little writer like me could benefit from some focus.

The thing I learned from him is that a mission statement doesn't just help you to *formulate* a focus, it helps you to *keep* that focus.

Almost every company I can think of has one. For example, Chick-fil-a's mission is, "Be America's best quick-service restaurant."

And their corporate purpose is, "To glorify God by being a faithful steward of all that is entrusted to us. To have a positive influence on all who come in contact with Chick-fil-A." *(taken from their website)*

That definitely gives the company a clear focus and sets them apart from every other fast food restaurant in town.

I can also see where this would be an asset to them. In the heat of a media storm they can stand strong holding to the original purpose on which they established the company.

In the same way a united purpose is an asset to a couple. Our faith is a stronghold when our marriage is threatened.

A couple is definitely stronger when they're clearly united with the same purpose and the same set of values.

This is where a mission statement might be an asset. I got this idea from my friend Ruth who created one for her family. I started looking around and thought, wait a minute, churches do this, big companies do this, bloggers do this, why don't marriages?

I loved the idea and couldn't wait to get started on one of my own. Would you like to make one too? If so, here's a basic outline.

Get together with your husband, pray about it first. Then have fun creating it together!

Part 1: Start with a mission

It can be one line or several. Ours is *"To have a Christ-centered marriage that brings glory to God through the way that we love and the way that we live. That we would be servants of grace who give more than we're given and forgive before we're forgiven."*
Put this on the mission statement in part 1. I encourage you to take this section of your statement and also copy it onto a small piece of paper that you can keep out in the open as a constant reminder. If you don't know what to write as your mission, feel free to use the one I have here.

Part 2: List your values

These are things that are important to you as a couple. For example, they might be items like going to bed together at the same time every night, getting up together every morning, turning the TV off at a certain time, and reading the Bible together every day.

Part 3: List your goals or dreams

This could include ideas like saving for college, retiring young, setting up a ministry, homeschooling your children, etc.

What's interesting about this section is that it can also become a source of prayer for your marriage as you dream about the future together.

The purpose of the mission statement is to keep you focused on those things that are important to your marriage and keep it free from distraction. Reflect on it often and bring it to prayer if you find that you're veering off track.

You might decide to change your mission in a year or so, and that's okay too. The important thing is that you keep your marriage focused on bringing glory to God.

S-O-A-P

Scripture

Read Philippians 3

Observation

What are some of your personal observations from this lesson?

Application

How can you apply this to your life?

Prayer

Dear Heavenly Father,

I pray that you will help us to grow with faith-focused determination. Help us to take off every weight of this world so that we might be used according to Your will. Guide us through planning our dreams and setting our mission with hearts that are focused on You. Amen.

LESSON FOUR

A SELF-CONTROLLED WIFE

Let us bring our affections into line with His, and, for the sake of His name, let us renounce the quest for worldly comforts and join His global purpose.

JOHN PIPER

THROUGHOUT SCRIPTURE WE SEE THE BATTLE of self-control described as an ongoing war between the spirit and flesh. Here is one of many scriptures that describes that war:

> *For the flesh lusteth against the Spirit, and the Spirit against the flesh: and these are contrary the one to the other: so that ye cannot do the things that ye would.*
>
> GALATIANS 5:17

Paul goes into great detail on the subject in Romans chapter 7:

> *For the good that I would I do not: but the evil which I would not, that I do.*
>
> ROMANS 7:19

The flesh is that voice in your head that tells you, "If it *feels* good do it." It tells us that we need things when we don't, and if we followed it we'd sleep too late, eat too much, and eventually come to poverty. That's where the heart wants to lead us.

The Spirit is the voice that tells you, "If it *is* good do it." The closer you walk with God, and the more time that you spend in His presence the more that you become aware of *His* will in your life.

His covenant is written upon our hearts and our minds, but there's a battle within each one of us. Satan wants to pull us away from our faith.

And how does he do that?

Most of the time it's with arguments that make a whole lot of sense in the moment, but in the long run they always lead to destruction.

Take Adam and Eve for example. They were given one commandment—only one. They could eat from every tree in the garden, but one was forbidden to them.

Satan is cunning. He came in the form of a serpent to tempt them to disobey God.

> *Eve said, "God hath said, Ye shall not eat of it, neither shall ye touch it, lest ye die."*
>
> GEN. 3:3

And the serpent said unto the woman,

> *"Ye shall not surely die: For God doth know that in the day ye eat thereof, then your eyes shall be opened, and ye shall be as gods, knowing good and evil."*
>
> GEN. 3:4-5

Part of that appeared to be true--they didn't die a *physical* death that day. They went on to live for many years, but the real truth of the matter is that they experienced a *spiritual* death the moment they chose to disobey. God doesn't lie, but scripture can be distorted and it can be twisted to fit our agenda.

The minute that something doesn't make sense to us, we want to figure out why. It's okay to be a deep thinker and to study the will of God. By all means, we should! But if we come to a cross road where we have to choose the wisdom of God over our ability to rationalize it, we must be willing to follow the Spirit.

If we're only obeying God when it makes sense to us then we're living to serve *ourselves*, not the Spirit. God's laws don't always make sense to us, quite often they require us to step out of our comfort zone or to feel the sting of refinement.

We live in a modern, self-centered society that encourages people to be happy at any cost. We're fed this idea that modern women are strong and in control because they do what they want, they say what they want, and they live anyway that they want to.

I came across an interesting article in the *New York Times* by John Tierney, called "A Generations Vanity Heard Through the Lyrics." He writes, *"After a computer analysis of three decades of hit songs, Dr. DeWall and other psychologists report finding what they were looking for: a statistically significant trend toward narcissism and hostility in popular music."*

Miley Cyrus recently came out with a song that peaked at #2 on the US Billboard's top 100, "Can't Stop." She sings:

> *Doing whatever we want*
> *This is our house*
> *This is our rules*

And we can't stop

And we won't stop...

She's right and she's wrong. Perhaps you *won't* stop, but the truth is that you *can* stop. That's what self-control is for.

Assuming that someone is strong because they do whatever they want to or whatever they *feel* like doing in the moment is foolish. It takes strength to bring your flesh under subjection to your spirit.

Have you ever found yourself opening up a second bag of chips or a candy bar because you just can't stop?

What about losing your cool and telling somebody off because you couldn't help it?

Maybe you're having a secret affair, and you can't break it off because you'll be physically sick if you do?

Whether we're getting up early to dig into the Word, controlling our appetite because it's the right thing to do, or breaking off a relationship that's detrimental to our marriage, we're going to feel the sting that comes with refinement.

The Bible compares the refinement of our faith to fire. It hurts. It stings. It's difficult to endure... But once you come out on the other side, you see that "joy unspeakable" is yours for the taking.

Temporal happiness could never compare to the inner peace that comes from serving the Lord!

There's an old Cherokee legend about two wolves at war. It's good food for thought on the topic of self-control.

One night a grandfather was teaching his grandson about life. "A fight is going on inside me," he said to the boy. "It is a terrible fight between two wolves. One is evil – he is anger, envy, sorrow, regret, greed, arrogance, self-pity, guilt, resentment, inferiority, lies, false pride, superiority, and ego." He continued,

"The other is good – he is joy, peace, love, hope, serenity, humility, kindness, benevolence, empathy, generosity, truth, compassion, and faith. The same fight is going on inside you – and inside every other person, too."

The boy paused to think for a moment before looking up at his grandfather. "Which wolf will win?" He asked.

The wise man simply replied, "The one that you feed."

Hearing that story, I'm reminded of the scripture that says,

> *And they that are Christ's have crucified the flesh with the affections and lusts.*
>
> GALATIANS 5:24

Those who walk in the Spirit walk according to the wisdom that they've been given. In other words, *they make choices day after day to put away sin.*

When we fall, we praise God for His unfailing grace, but we stand up again and get back in the race.

Putting away sin starts with a decision, and then it calls for self-control. Unless we're convicted however, we might just stay where we are.

Here's an example. During my twenties I started struggling with my weight. I went from a 98 pound bride to a 150 pound 30-something-year-old within ten years. I'm short so the extra bit of weight was uncomfortable and I was into plus-sized clothing. I tried everything to take off the weight, but nothing would stick.

Self-control didn't work. I mean it did for a while, but it never had the long-lasting affect I was looking for.

One day it hit me. The problem? I wasn't convicted. I'd go for about three days controlling my appetite, but the moment the arguments set in (and they always did) I had nothing to fall back on, aside from the fact that I wanted to lose a few pounds. There wasn't any valid reason I could think of for sticking to the plan.

That is until I started to study God's Word. I mean *really* dig in. After finishing the Bible, I read it again, and again, and again... then I went to the Greek and read that again and again. I must have gone through the entire Bible about 6-8 times that year. I was hungry for the Word, but more importantly I was *convicted*.

Scripture after scripture talked about the virtue of self-control. It talked about controlling our appetites, about greed, and how our bodies are temples of the Holy Ghost. It talked about crucifying the flesh and anything else that controls you.

There isn't anything wrong with eating chips at 2:00 am, but the question to ask yourself is, do you control your appetite or does it control you?

Here's a little wisdom from Paul. He's talking about the freedom we have in Christ:

> *"Everything is permissible for me–but not everything is beneficial. Everything is permissible for me–but I will not be mastered by anything."*
>
> 1 CORINTHIANS 6:12, NIV

The same could be said about anything in your life. Ask yourself if *you're* in control, or if you're *being* controlled.

We serve a God Who wants our adoration; He wants our love; and He wants our hearts in their entirety. If we are mastered by the things of this world, we're sharing our heart with another.

That deep conviction was life-changing for me. I lost 40 pounds and kept if off for over a decade. Day after day, I made wise choices and I kept making wise choices even when the going was tough.

Why I'm overweight now is a combination of two things. One is that I have this crazy medication for my tremors that slows down my body. I'm exhausted most of the time and all I want to do is sleep. Without it I shake. Even my legs tremble when I'm standing in a line-up. One year I was exercising every day, the next I was struggling just to stay awake.

The other reason—and this is of most importance to me—is that this conviction hasn't been as real to me as it once was. I've let this area of my life slip. I know that if I get back to exercising every day that I'll have more energy, and I know that eating better and drinking less caffeine will make a difference too. Like Paul says in Romans 7:15, *"For what I would, that do I not; but what I hate, that do I."*

This is an area of my life that I need to give up to God. I need to trust His wisdom that says, *everything is permissible, but not everything is beneficial.* I need to exercise this virtue until my Spirit is ruling the flesh. Maybe I can't do everything I used to do, but I definitely can make some changes.

This isn't easy to talk about. It's embarrassing in fact. But the truth is that appetite is a struggle so many of us are wrestling with.

We know what is good, what is right, and what is best for our bodies, but day after day we follow the lust of the flesh that leads to more junk in the trunk.

The bottom line is that you're not struggling with food. You're struggling with self-control. Your flesh is at war with your Spirit.

Which one will win?

The one that you feed.

As for you skinny girls, you're not off the hook. The same principle applies to each and every one of us, as we struggle with self-control in different areas. If we're not ruled by the Spirit we're being ruled by the flesh.

And so we see that the fruit of self-control is the result of a person who is walking in virtue by making daily decisions to put down the flesh. She's equipped with wisdom, and she's down on her knees in prayer.

A virtuous woman isn't ruled by her passions, she passionately pursues an incomparable God. She is strong because she knows that she can do what she wants, but she chooses to do that which is good.

As I'm writing this, I feel the hand of God gently tug on my heart. He's speaking to me as He's speaking to you. These words aren't solely for the purpose of writing, but rather that the reader as well as the author will take them to heart. Draw closer to Him, exercise virtue, and start changing today.

S-O-A-P

Scripture
Read Romans 7

Observation
What are some of your personal observations from this lesson?

Application
How can you apply this to your life?

Prayer
Dear Heavenly Father,

Please help me to be self-controlled in every area of my life. Guide me in understanding Your will for my marriage and grant me the strength and wisdom to choose it.

More of you, Lord. Less of me. Amen.

LESSON FIVE

A Trustworthy Wife

Make your heart a safe place for his.

LISA JACOBSON

HAVE YOU EVER WONDERED WHY YOU'RE SO relaxed around some people and others you're not? Ever notice how some friends bring you down into a state of depression while others lift you up? Have you ever been to a party and noticed that when one person gets up to leave the others start leaving too?

Whether we are aware of this fact or not, we tend to mirror the actions of people around us. A perfect example of this is when a friend orders dessert, and we say "Why not—I'll have dessert too!"

In the same way, we often mirror the negative behavior of those around us without realizing it.

Thinking back I recall a few times when a friend has offered a piece of gossip to me and all the while she was talking I was thinking of something I could share in return.

It's been the same way when it comes to talking about our husbands. A friend might say, "I was so mad at Justin last night, because I told him..."

And without thinking about it, I'll chime in and say, "Oh, Michael does that too!! It drives me crazy." And then we get into a discussion that unearths every fault I can dig up from 25 years of observation and put a negative spin on it.

I've been there, done that, and I regret every word that I've said.

I believe that most of us gossip to gain a feeling of superiority. We don't want people to view us as inferior, so we verbally lower others in an attempt to elevate ourselves.

In the Old Testament, several negative words are used to describe a gossip, which can be translated as: backbiter, slanderer, talebearer, and whisperer.

Bottom line is that gossip is more than just asking about the weather—it's laced with malicious intent. It's tattling when you shouldn't. It's telling secrets that should be kept private. And yes—it's finding fault in your husband and sharing those details with a friend over tea.

I don't care how nice her smile is or how many pats she gives you on the back. If the conversation isn't for the purpose of edification, correction, or instruction we need to control our tongue to ensure that our conversation doesn't dishonor our marriage or more importantly *our walk with the Lord.*

> *Make it your ambition to lead a quiet life: You should mind your own business and work with your hands, just as we told you, so that your daily life may win the respect of outsiders and so that you will not be dependent on anybody.*
>
> 1 THESSALONIANS 4:11-12, NIV

See what that says? "Win the respect of outsiders." It's really ironic when you think about it. The intent of our gossip is to elevate ourselves, but it really does the exact opposite. Every time an ugly word comes out of our mouth, we are losing the respect of the listener.

So how do we stop?

If your tongue has been babbling on for several years, consider it a wild horse. You need to tame that horse by training it thought-by-thought and word-by-word, taking every thought captive, until you're willing to yield to the obedience of Christ. Only then will you respond to the bridle.

> *For in many things we offend all. If any man offend not in word, the same is a perfect man, and able also to bridle the whole body.*
>
> JAMES 3:2, KJV

Practice bringing your thoughts into subjection *before* they roll off your tongue. Then you can honor your husband by being his cheerleader and trustworthy companion when he's home or when he's out of your sight.

There's a quote that reads, "Love the people God gave you, because he will need them back one day." – Unknown.

Reading that, I couldn't help but be reminded of The Parable of the Talents in which a master went on a journey leaving a sum of gold with each of his servants. Upon his return, the master discovered that two of the servants wisely invested the gold, while the third servant hid his bag of gold in the ground.

To the faithful he gave more, and from the foolish, he took back what was given and gave it to the other two servants.

We're all given proverbial bags of gold in this life. For me few are as precious as my husband and children. This marriage, this home and everything in it is on loan to me for a season. When I invest in their lives, I invest in the Master.

S-O-A-P

Scripture
Read Matthew 25:14-28

Observation
What are some of your personal observations from this lesson?

Application
How can you apply this to your life?

Prayer
Dear Heavenly Father,

Teach me to be a safe place for my husband. To hold his heart as a treasure that's not to be toyed with or used for my pleasure. Thank you for the gift of a wonderful husband. I pray that I'll invest each and every day for Your glory. Amen.

LESSON SIX

AN ENCOURAGING WIFE

*No one is useless in this world who lightens the
burdens of another.*

CHARLES DICKENS

DARKNESS ENVELOPED THE SKY DRAWING ITS curtain around us,
while the rumble of thunder composed a symphony of sound
that was carried by on the wings of the wind.

It was only 8 pm, but Michael was fast asleep. Stretched
out on his recliner by the window, he dozed off while two little
puppies wrestled under his chair.

The steady tip-tapping of rain made me want to curl up
beside him and fall asleep too, but I had some dishes that needed
to be cleared away and some laundry to do for the morning.

I wasn't surprised to see him sleeping like that. I knew he'd
be exhausted after the crazy week he just had. Working overtime
every night, he was struggling to catch up at work.

And the weekend? It wasn't much better. Since he's been at
the shop so much lately, the honey-do list was long and he was
determined to get it all done.

He's a hard worker, there's no doubt about that. And weeks like this remind me of just how hard he pushes himself when the going gets tough.

There's a lot of weight on that man's shoulders. In fact, I can say that about most husbands I know. Even when they aren't facing deadlines at work, they are dealing with the spiritual and financial responsibilities that come with leading a family.

While many of them appear to have everything under control, most of our husbands would not only appreciate encouragement from us, they would benefit from it.

Any mom who cares for a growing child knows the importance of praise in their children's life. Not only does it help to build a healthy sense of self-esteem, it also reminds a child that he or she is loved.

In the same way, any wife who cares for her husband will also know the importance of praise in a marriage. It's vital to a growing relationship.

In "103 Words of Affirmation Every Husband Wants to Hear," Matthew L. Jacobson writes, *"We need your affirmation – we have to have it and, oh, how we thrive with it. Typically, men are quiet about these things but that doesn't mean we need and enjoy our wife's affirmation any less. And every man feels it: When his woman is behind him, he can slay dragons."*

Do you realize that there are four verses in Proverbs alone that talk about nagging wives? They are referred to as quarrelsome, fretful, and a continual dripping. If you have ever experienced a leaky roof, you'll know how annoying that is. We experienced one about 20 years ago in our back porch, and regardless of how many times I emptied the pail it would only fill up again.

That's the danger with nagging. It becomes a never-ending habit if left unchecked, and unfortunately it festers resentment. Praise on the other hand has the reverse affect. It builds the bond of marriage and draws a couple closer together.

That's only two of the benefits, but there are so many more. Let's look at five of them:

1. When you affirm him, you are affirming your adoration of him. Knowing that someone loves you deeply strengthens the bond of marriage. Think of it this way: we form the strongest friendships with those that we deeply trust.

2. When you praise him for the little things he does, it's more likely that he'll be encouraged to repeat them in the future.

3. When I praise my husband, whether it be in his presence or in his absence, we bear witness of our marriage covenant. Keeping in mind that marriage reflects the covenant between Jesus Christ and the church it's important to honor our vows in the best way we know how.

4. Kindness is an attractive quality. There's no possible way a wife can be attractive when she's constantly nagging her husband. Sure, you can put the pretty on, but unless you're also attractive it wears thin. There's nothing appealing about a critical spirit.

5. He'll be glad to come home. Let's face it, the world is tough place. Many of our husbands are dealing with difficult situations at work and need a sense of relief when they walk through the door. Unfortunately, some other husbands are working with women who are

building them up outside of the home. If we want a husband who is glad to come home to his wife, we can make him feel welcome by letting him know that we appreciate him, that we respect him, and that we're glad he is with us.

Here are a Few Do's and Don'ts for Every Encouraging Wife to Keep in Mind:

Do remember that a man's qualities run deeper than the surface work that we see. Whether he has had a productive day or he's kicking back and relaxing, he possesses certain qualities that make him unique. Some of Michael's qualities are that he's a giving person. He's a good listener. He's hungry for the Word of God. He's a man of grace. He's sensitive. etc. Encourage your husband by affirming his own unique character.

Don't take his gifts of love for granted. Does he do little jobs around the house for you? Thank him, even if you look at it as his responsibility. My husband has thanked me for cleaning up every time I do, which means that he's probably thanked me about 8,670 times. Yes, he thanks me daily.

Do take time to listen to him about his day and hear what he's saying. Michael will say to me, "I'm sorry to unload on you, but there's no one else I can talk to about this…" That makes me wonder how many men out there feel the same way. Do they have someone they can talk to about work issues? Hopefully you will be there to listen and encourage him.

Do share his burden. Offer to help him out when he's having a busy week. Is there anything you can do to pitch in? Maybe take on a chore you don't normally do? If so he might appreciate the help and the company.

Don't be the nag who rains on his parade–be the smile that brightens his day. If women didn't have a tendency to nag like we do, the Bible wouldn't reference it as often as it does. Unfortunately, it can become a bad habit if we don't learn to control our tongue. Joy on the other hand is encouraging and contagious. Work on keeping a positive attitude not only for yourself, but for the good of your family.

Don't expect him to be your savior. Your husband isn't Jesus, therefore he isn't perfect, he can't read your mind, he will disappoint you at times, and he doesn't have the patience of Job. He's simply a man growing in grace and learning to lead. Praise God for the husband you have, imperfections and all.

Do take time to pray for your husband every day. Ask him if there's anything he wants you to pray about, and let him know that you're praying. There's nothing more encouraging than knowing that someone is praying you through a situation.

S-O-A-P

Scripture
Read Genesis 2:15-25

Observation
What are some of your personal observations from this lesson?

Application
How can you apply this to your life?

Prayer
Dear Heavenly Father,

I pray that I will be an encouragement to my husband, and that I'll be steadfast in prayer and equipped with love. Help me to see past the man that I expect him to be and to gain focus of the man that he is. Amen.

LESSON SEVEN

A PURE WIFE

Purity is to live according to original design.

JOSH MCDOWELL

I WENT DOWN TO MY LAUNDRY room the other day, and after pushing my way through the door I said to myself, *this mountain of laundry—it has to be a direct result of the curse.*

And then I got to thinking about Adam and Eve and how they didn't wear clothes before they bit into the fruit. It was only *after* sin entered the world that laundry was heaped upon them.

I think about Gideon's family. We're told in Judges that he had seventy sons, which makes for a lot of laundry regardless of how many wives the man had.

It's never ending isn't it? That and dishes. My sister once told me that a happy woman is one whose dishes and laundry are done. She has a good point.

Just one month ago I was all caught up. The laundry was finished, it was folded, and all put away. Then I went on vacation with my daughter for four days. FOUR DAYS is all it took to get back out of control. Then Christmas happened, then major renovations, and… well… it's not pretty let me tell you. I'll be doing laundry until the cows come home every day this week.

Looking back on the years I see a lot of similarities here. Love isn't something we can fold up nicely and place into a drawer for safe keeping. It's something we put on every single day, and the reality is that we mess it up all the time. Impatience, resentment, and pride have a way of working themselves into our marriage.

The easy thing to do is to sit back and hope that our dirty laundry washes itself, but the *right* thing to do is to purify our hearts in obedience to God's word and continue to purify our hearts every day.

> *Therefore, since we have these promises, dear friends, let us purify ourselves from everything that contaminates body and spirit, perfecting holiness out of reverence for God.*
>
> 2 CORINTHIANS 7:1

Choosing to follow your sin puts you in a dangerous place where Satan has a foothold in your marriage. If we allow resentment to grow, it will grow, and if we allow our hearts to harden toward the one that we love it will become calloused over time.

Most importantly, the goal of each and every one of us should be that of bringing glory to God both today and every day of our lives.

When we consider the idea of purity, the first thing that usually comes to mind is one's sexuality. By protecting our purity, we save ourselves for marriage.

That's an important step for every single Christian to take, but there are many ways that we are called to purity, and several ways that we exercise the virtue of purity in our lives long after we say, "I do."

In the Bible we often see purification as being a ceremonial cleansing. For example, Esther went through a purification process before she was presented to the king, and in Numbers chapter 8, we see that Moses and Aaron purified the Levites and they washed their clothes before they served in the tabernacle.

For Christians today, purification takes place in the heart and soul. In First Peter 1:22 we see that we purify our hearts by obeying the truth. It's a matter of keeping our lives and our thoughts free from sin.

But the cleansing is two-fold. First and foremost, we are purified spiritually through faith in Jesus Christ.

> *If we confess our sins, he is faithful and just to forgive us our sins and to cleanse us from all unrighteousness.*
>
> 1 JOHN 1:9

What we're focusing on in this chapter however is exercising the *virtue* of purity–an act of obedience that follows repentance. It's a matter of embracing the goodness of God, and it's one of the many ways that we glorify Him with our life.

The fact that God is holy, pure, righteous, and good should be evident through the lives of His people. And if we're not reflecting the goodness of God, what message are we sending the world about who He is?

When something is pure, it's free from toxins and contamination, just as our lives and our thoughts should be free from all that's unholy.

Scripture after scripture tells us to take our thoughts captive, to keep our bodies from sin, and to guard our hearts according to the Word.

We all know that the smallest temptation can turn into sin and take root when we allow it to step through the door. Just one look, just one thought, just one email, just one day...

> *Be sober, be vigilant; because your adversary the devil, as a roaring lion, walketh about, seeking whom he may devour.*
>
> 1 PETER 5:8

Purity begins the moment we make a decision to choose well. When we stand up to the flesh and follow the spirit. The minute we take a thought captive and bring it into obedience to Christ, we are exercising the virtue of purity.

Purity stems from the heart. Our bodies are merely an instrument of the heart. The way that we use them depends upon the choices we make.

The best way to calm that war within is by guarding our heart according to the Word of God.

> *Above all else, guard your heart, for everything you do flows from it.*
>
> PROVERBS 4:23

We can also exercise this virtue is by correction. When we see ourselves slipping into old habits we can stop right there and remind ourselves that this isn't the way we want things to go down.

I've done this aloud in front of my own family at times. I start telling them something and then halfway through a sentence I've realized that I'm not making the best choice, so I stop and correct myself.

Whether I'm gossiping about someone, telling a lie, or being insensitive in the way that I speak it's important that I stop it as soon as I can.

It's so much easier to catch it *before* it comes out of your mouth isn't it? That's why prayer is so important to change. It helps to put our heart in line with God's will and invites Him to work alongside us.

Jesus said,

> *"For my yoke is easy and my burden is light."*
>
> MATTHEW 11:30

> *Take my yoke upon you and learn from me, for I am gentle and humble in heart, and you will find rest for your souls.*
>
> MATTHEW 11:29, NIV

What Jesus is asking us to do is to walk in step with him. He uses the analogy of a yoke here, which is a piece of wood that is fastened to the neck of a pair of oxen. When one turns, the other turns, when one stops, the other stops too. In a way it's like following someone who is leading a dance.

We don't always know which steps to take at first and there are days when we're stepping on toes, but when we trust in our partner and follow *His* lead we watch and we learn until the dance becomes second nature to us.

The Pure in Heart

Another term for the virtue of purity is "pure in heart." To be pure in heart means to have *good intentions*. The opposite of that would be doing good merely because we feel *obligated* to, or doing one thing while thinking another, otherwise labeled as a hypocrite.

I remember driving in the car one evening with my oldest son. We had just come back from a meeting where a couple of the women infuriated me.

"I'm not like that." I said to Brendan, "I'd never been so rude to a person..."

As far as I was concerned, I was a good girl. I held my tongue. I didn't shake things up like I could have. I never would. I'm too kind for that type of behavior.

At least I *thought* I was, until I heard Brendan's response. He sharpened and challenged me with his wisdom when he said, "Not really. It's not that you're any kinder than them–you're just too shy to really say what's on your mind."

Ouch. That comment stung, but his words rang true and I knew it.

I had just spent ten minutes ragging on about these women and saying how much they got on my nerves. I hadn't stopped to consider that my *thoughts* were every bit as nasty as someone's actions could be.

I'm timid, and I'm shy, but I'm as guilty as the next when it comes to my thoughts.

I was reminded of the Pharisees who Jesus often reprimanded in scripture. He compared them to a cup that is clean on the outside, but dirty on the inside (see Matt. 23:25), and white-washed tombs:

> *Woe unto you, scribes and Pharisees, hypocrites! For ye are like unto whited sepulchres, which indeed appear beautiful outward, but are within full of dead men's bones, and of all uncleanness. 28 Even so ye also*

*outwardly appear righteous unto men, but within ye are
full of hypocrisy and iniquity.*

MATTHEW 23:27-28

God searches the heart; He sees the ugly parts that I tuck away
from the world. This is why it's important to consider my
thoughts as much as I do my actions.

Are they reflecting the love of Christ? Or do they reflect a
self-centered impatient heart?

A pure heart is one that is centered on Christ. She's a woman
who's walking in love, forgiving as Christ forgave her. She
exercises kind, compassionate love that's seasoned with grace.

I want to be that woman. Whether I'll ever get there I don't
know, but I do know that that I'm a work in progress who's
willing to exercise virtue day after day.

Are you with me on this? Let's look at four ways by which
we can grow:

1. **Consider your words.** This includes swearing, lying,
   gossiping, yelling, and bragging. Are you seeking to
   edify others? Is your conduct in-line with God's will? If
   it isn't, practice stopping yourself the moment it comes
   out of your mouth and correcting your behavior.

2. **Consider your love.** Do you love in order to *receive*
   love? Is the love you have toward your husband and God
   conditional? In other words, will you love them just as
   much tomorrow if life doesn't go your way?

   When love becomes just a matter of give and take we
   discover that some days we can't give because we haven't
   been given enough. Our love tank is empty. But if we
   love others simply because God loved us, we always have

our love tanks full by His Spirit, overflowing and ready to pour out on others.

Timothy Keller writes, *"Without the help of the Spirit, without a continual refilling of your soul's tank with the glory and love of the Lord, such submission to the interests of the other is virtually impossible to accomplish for any length of time without becoming resentful."* The Meaning of Marriage: Facing the Complexities of Commitment With the Wisdom of God.

3. **Consider your actions.** Are you serving others joyfully or grudgingly?

When we give from the heart as unto the Lord, anything we do including dishes starts to makes sense. We can say, "Lord, this is the job You have given me. These are the people You've entrusted into my care. And I'm going to serve them the best way I know how."

A virtuous woman understands that her final reward comes from the Lord.

4. **Consider your sexual behavior, and yes–your thoughts.** Is your desire to your own husband or toward another man?

But I say unto you, that whosoever looks on a woman to lust after her has committed adultery with her already in his heart.

MATTHEW 5:28

This pertains every bit as much to us as it does to the men.

It might seem harmless to hoot and howl over Hollywood's hottest hunk, but that kind of behavior isn't becoming of virtuous women because it isn't in step with God's desire for us. Men are created in the image of God and should be treated as such.

5. **Consider your intentions.** For example, if you are involved in ministry are you doing it for the sake of the Lord or is there a selfish reason you're doing it, such as winning the approval and praise of your peers?

Also consider your small acts of ministry like visiting a sick person in the hospital, bringing a meal to a family in need, babysitting for a friend in need, etc. The same question should be asked, "Why are you doing it--for the sake of the Lord or for your glory?"

S-O-A-P

Scripture

Read 1 John 1

Observation

What are some of your personal observations from this lesson?

Application

How can you apply this to your life?

Prayer

Dear Heavenly Father,

Give me the wisdom to exercises kindness and compassionate love that's seasoned with grace.

Purify my heart. And give me the strength to be refined into the woman I was created to be. Amen.

LESSON EIGHT

A LOVING WIFE

Love is a path paved with compassion and grace.

DARLENE SCHACHT

IN HIS BOOK, *THE FOUR LOVES*, C.S. Lewis writes, "Agape love is the highest level of love known to humanity, a selfless love, a love that is passionately committed to the well-being of others."

It's the highest level of love because it's the one that reflects God's gift to mankind through His Son Jesus Christ.

For God so loved the world, that he gave his only begotten Son, that whosoever believeth in him should not perish, but have everlasting life. – John 3:16

There's a key ingredient in agape love which is often forgotten by mankind, but never forgotten by God.

It's grace.

Without grace love becomes a barter system where we give as much as we're given and forgive only when we're forgiven.

When love is seasoned with grace it reaches down to people who deserve it the least because they need it the most. It serves the other on the good days and bad.

This goes against our modern way of thinking which says that love is 50/50 and that it has to go both ways. That way of thinking isn't love for another--it's love that's looking out for itself.

One of the best and most beautiful examples of agape love is illustrated through the devotion of parents with a newborn child. They come into this world fully reliant on us, not able to reciprocate in any way, and needing to be cared for in every way.

It's a one-way street that's more fulfilling than any other kind of love because it reflects the perfect love of God.

> *But God shows his love for us in that while we were still sinners, Christ died for us.*
>
> ROMANS 5:8

God's plan for marriage is perfect in every way. He designed both men and women to love each other more than we love ourselves.

Yes, it should go both ways. And isn't it nice when it does? Absolutely. But we can't let someone else's lack of character define who we are.

If we want to be virtuous women of strength then we must pattern our lives after our Savior who won the victory over sin and death.

If we say to ourselves, "He's bitter, therefore I'm bitter." We're choosing to walk after the flesh.

If we say, "He's selfish, therefore I'm selfish." We're choosing sin over the righteousness of Christ.

But if we can say to ourselves, "I love others because God loves me." We're choosing the higher road which is paved with forgiveness and grace.

Does this mean our husbands are off-the-hook, or that they don't have to take responsibility for their actions toward us? Absolutely not. Scripture clearly teaches that men are to love their wives as Christ loved the church and gave Himself up for it. They are both called to sacrificial love in the marriage.

Pastors, teachers, and preachers are constantly reminding them to walk in love. But if they choose to turn their ear away from the truth they will be judged accordingly.

Our responsibility is to keep our eyes on the Father and walk in His ways.

You can't fulfill your husband's role in this marriage, but you can fulfill your own.

You can't force another person to be who you want him to be but you can affect his heart by the way that you live. And let's not forget that we can be effective through prayer.

We find in scripture, love is the greatest virtue:

> *And now abides faith, hope, love, these three; but the greatest of these is love.*
>
> 1 CORINTHIANS 13:13

In addition to love being the greatest virtue, it is the most important commandment as it sums up God's deepest will for our lives:

> *Master, which is the great commandment in the law? 37 Jesus said unto him, Thou shalt love the Lord thy God with all thy heart, and with all thy soul, and with all thy mind. 38 This is the first and great commandment. 39 And the second is like unto it, Thou shalt love thy neighbor as thyself. 40 On these two commandments hang all the law and the prophets.*
>
> MATTHEW 22:36-40

As we see in this scripture, love is more than merely having affection for God and our fellow man; it's a willingness to lay down our lives for the sake of our Lord and to put our own desires aside for the good of our neighbor.

How is this reflected in the virtuous life of a Christ-centered wife?

The choices she makes reflect a heart that is abandoned to Christ.

She's willing to say,

My body, mind and spirit are Yours Lord. May I be used as an instrument of Your peace. Should my passions or desires dare to stand in my way, may they be crucified so that I might serve You above anything else.

She knows that serving the Lord is a beautiful thing, and that service calls her to walk in humility esteeming others higher than herself. Her love for God and man is the driving force behind the choices she makes.

Being equal to her husband, she is not in competition with him. She is ready and willing to step down in order that he might lead their family as scripture commands him.

> *Wives, submit yourselves unto your own husbands, as unto the Lord. 23 For the husband is the head of the wife, even as Christ is the head of the church: and he is the saviour of the body.*
> EPHESIANS 5:23-24

She is driven by love.

She makes every effort to be patient and kind with her husband giving all diligence to understanding his heart. She's a vessel of love that's pouring out grace both in and outside of the home.

Her charity stems from a heart of compassion that reaches out to the world. Her hands and her feet are messengers of the gospel, bringing good news of God's love to mankind.

She's not arrogant or selfish or rude, because she's defined by the grace of God and nothing less.

> *I am crucified with Christ: nevertheless I live; yet not I, but Christ liveth in me: and the life which I now live in the flesh I live by the faith of the Son of God, who loved me, and gave himself for me.*
>
> GALATIANS 2:20

She's not perfect. In fact she has days like anyone else where she feels the weight of the world on her shoulders. She wonders how she could fail so miserably, why she doesn't measure up to the other women around her, and how God could possibly love her on those days when she can't love herself.

That's when God reminds her of His unfailing grace and how He loved her before she loved Him.

Everything we have, everything we are, and everything we do is God's gift of grace upon our lives.

He's not looking for perfection—we've already been perfected by grace.

S-O-A-P

Scripture
Read 1 Corinthians 13

Observation
What are some of your personal observations from this lesson?

Application
How can you apply this to your life?

Prayer
Dear Heavenly Father,

Teach me to love the way you love--with patience, and kindness, and grace. Help me to love well on the good days and bad. You have given me much to be thankful for, Lord. May Your Holy Spirit guide me to shine as a light in this dark world—keeping in step with Your will. Amen.

LESSON NINE

A PATIENT WIFE

*Good character is not formed in a week or a month. It is
created little by little, day by day. Protracted and patient effort
is needed to develop good character.*

HERACLITUS

THE YEAR WAS 1989. IT WAS our second year of marriage, and we
set up house on the eleventh floor of a twelve story apartment
building.

I remember being second from the top. The man who lived
above us liked to bang the life out of his balcony railing, while
kicking and screaming at the top his lungs.

It was therapy, we were told. He needed an outlet to vent
his frustration and the balcony was the closest thing he had to
an open field.

It didn't bother us so much as it humored us. And since he
only vented while the sun was up we weren't losing any sleep.

We were however losing sleep over a completely different
matter.

The rock band Guns N' Roses released a hit song that year
called "Patience." I was never a Guns N' Roses fan, but I came

to like the song. The gentle ballad starts out with Axl Rose whistling the tune accompanied by three acoustic guitars.

"Shed a tear cause I'm missing you, I'm still alright to smile... all we need is just a little patience."

It was catchy. Everyone at work was whistling the tune and every kid with a guitar was picking out the melody–including our next door neighbors.

Technically they weren't next door. They lived across the hall from us, and from what I could tell our bathroom vents were somehow connected. I'd often hear them playing guitar while I was curling my hair or brushing my teeth. From the sounds of it, they only knew one song, which they played over and over again.

Being a musician, you'd think my husband would enjoy it. But he didn't. Like water wearing down a rock, the constant strum of their guitar and the boom, boom, boom from their stereo got under his skin.

I remember lying in bed at night sound asleep. Michael would sit up and say, "What's that sound?"

I couldn't hear anything at all, but apparently he could hear music and it was driving him crazy--so crazy that we finally moved out.

Isn't it ironic that "patience" is the very thing that got under his skin?

That's how life is though isn't it? When something is troubling us we want it resolved as soon as possible. The trying of our patience is one of the most difficult tasks for us to endure, but it builds character in those who are exercised by it.

In Romans chapter five, Paul writes,

> *By whom also we have access by faith into this grace wherein we stand, and rejoice in hope of the glory of*

*God. And not only so, but we glory in tribulations also:
knowing that tribulation worketh patience; and patience,
experience; and experience, hope.*

ROMANS 5: 2-4

Guitars playing at 2 in the morning–that's nothing really. But serious tribulation, the kind that rips through your home, leaving you discouraged and dismayed calls for incredible patience as we cling to the Lord for a sense of peace.

This level of patience doesn't come easy, but it is a virtue that we can exercise day in and day out.

There's a constant call to patience in every one of our lives.

It can be anything from the way we present ourselves in rush hour traffic to the way we handle our emotions when we disagree with our husband.

A kind word goes a long way in diffusing an argument. We might we feel like our opinion needs to be expressed right then and there regardless of his emotions, but having a little patience and waiting for an opportune time to bring up the discussion again might be a wiser decision.

Are we holding our tempers? Are we biting our tongues? Are we looking at life with a glass half-full of grace?

Practicing the little things prepare us for the bigger things in life.

Patience in circumstance is important, but what's equally important is that a husband and wife learn to be patient with each other.

Michael is not perfect, but trying to change him has never been effective, and vice versa. Working to transform *ourselves* however, has changed the way we both live and the way that we love.

Living with another person isn't so easy–I learned that 40 years ago when I shared a bed with my sister.

Patience is holding your temper when you're angry, and biting your tongue when you're about to say something you shouldn't.

I'm reminded of those earlier years when computers were new. Some days I thought they were ridiculous and other days I wanted nothing more than to toss them aside and go back to the old way of doing things. Paper and pen made sense, windows and programs didn't.

I can't tell you how many nights I spent on the telephone with technicians trying to figure out how to perform the most basic functions----one of which involved simply turning the computer off and turning it back on. *Who knew?!*

Ever minimize a window and exclaim, "Oh no! What did I do?!" Yeah, that was me.

It wasn't until I understood computers and had a little experience with them that I finally learned to fully appreciate their value. Now I get it. I still need my kid's to help me now and then, but I appreciate everything that one little machine can do.

Patience was a necessary virtue in learning and growing.

In the same way there have been frustrating days when like thousands of women around me, I wanted to give up on my marriage with Michael–times when I've seen his imperfections and he has seen mine; times when "glorious without limit" seemed challenging without end. Thrive or survive—the choice was ours.

We're complicated. It takes patience and time to understand each other and to fully appreciate our value.

Instead of giving up, we dug our heels in and stood firm. We held onto our marriage with a fierce grip. We saw the way that patience and grace can affect a marriage, while bringing glory and honor to God. It was good!

I write this book with a message of hope—don't discard something so precious. When we learn to respect, honor and cherish our spouse the way *God* wants us to love, marriages are transformed.

Husbands treat us differently when we treasure the men that they are, and we respond better to them when they lovingly cherish us back.

> *With all lowliness and meekness, with longsuffering, forbearing one another in love; Endeavouring to keep the unity of the Spirit in the bond of peace.*
>
> EPHESIANS 4:2-3

Patience is a virtue that must be exercised if we ever hope to mature.

The best example of this is found in scripture when Jesus prayed on the cross. "Father, forgive them," He said, "For they know not what they do."

He had every reason to be angry, spiteful, impatient, and hostile, but He chose patience, forgiveness, and grace.

Life can be hard, but our marriage is never past hope.

There is no such thing as hopeless when our eyes are fixed on God. God transforms the impossible into the possible. He offers the unpromising a promise. He gives strength to the weak. He encourages the discouraged. There isn't one troubled marriage that God cannot fix.

Is anything too hard for the Lord? Absolutely not!

Don't give up too quickly. Don't quit too soon, lest you leave before the harvest comes in.

I have seen the harvest that times of patience has brought, and with sincerity of heart I tell you: it is good–very good!

The Daffodil Garden

Have you ever heard the story of the daffodil garden?

The beauty of the garden holds a lesson to be learned. Let me tell it to you my way…

In 1958, (Alma) Gene and Dale Bauer started planting a garden of daffodils, planting them one by one by one… throughout the years. Today the daffodil garden in Running Springs, California is said to be the largest daffodil garden in the world. One look at the magnificent hillside immediately draws you in. Google it and you'll see!

This mountain hillside, which was once a wilderness of poor rocky soil is now drenched with daffodils. A breath-taking experience to the tourists it draws.

The countless daffodils reflect care, as stewards of God's creation, labor in the land they've been given. Man and woman, side by side. But the unmistakable miracle we see—made by the hands of only two—is that perseverance yields fruit to those who are trained by it.

Gene Bauer planted the first 48 bulbs in 1958, describing her persistence by saying, "One at a time, by one woman. Two hands, two feet and a body minus a brain." In forty years she's planted close to a million bulbs!

The daffodil garden illustrates the God given potential that each one of us holds when we plant seeds one by one: seeds of discipline, love, joy, peace, patience, goodness, faith, meekness, and self-control—seeds that will blossom in our garden one day, a breath-taking garden that draws others to Christ.

In 1988, my husband and I planted a garden of love when we stood at the altar, saying, "I do."

It's been 24 years of planting one bulb at a time--nothing too big, just one bloom here and there among countless flowers.

One prayer at a time, one day at a time, one understanding and patient moment at a time… precious blooms in the garden of marriage.

Want to exercise patience? Let's look at five ways to do that today:

1. **Ride the burn.** We all want instant gratification, and when we don't get it we feel the burn. I don't know if you're anything like me, but I can feel a physical reaction when I'm exercising patience and it's uncomfortable. Say for example I'm angry at a friend and I desperately want to vent my frustration. My heart races and my head spins. Kind of like when I can't have the extra calories I want.

   It's like an internal temper tantrum. But what it really comes down to is that my spirit is at war with my flesh. Ride it out and it will go away. Once you're thinking clearly, you can respond wisely.

2. **Pray without ceasing.** Prayer is not a last resort—it's the first and most important destination of any journey that we take. Some people only go to God when they're desperate, others are desperate to seek Him every day.

   Never under-estimate the power that He holds to not only change a situation, but to create an outcome that's beyond anything you could imagine for yourself.

3. **Grab a pen and paper.** Pull out a journal and start writing down some of the scriptures on patience. Look them up online or in a concordance and see where God is speaking to you.

4. **Remind yourself that you're developing character.** This one is key, and the reason why is because your attitude will not be dependent on the attitude of another. Don't mirror the impatient actions of those around you. Keep your eyes on Jesus. Consider the patience and persistence that He had and strive to be like Him alone.

5. **Ask yourself how you can glorify God.** You might have a split second to ask this question, but the more you get used to asking it, the more it will come naturally to you. Ask yourself how you can glorify God in this situation and remind yourself that this life is not about you. That's a difficult one to remember, but when we consider that everything we do is for the glory of God, attitudes change.

My brethren, count it all joy when ye fall into divers temptations; knowing this, that the trying of your faith worketh patience. But let patience have her perfect work, that ye may be perfect and entire, wanting nothing.

JAMES 1:2-4

S-O-A-P

Scripture

Read Job 1

Observation

What are some of your personal observations from this lesson?

Application

How can you apply this to your life?

Prayer

Dear Heavenly Father,

Thank you for the many times that You've been patient with me. I hope in the same way that I'll learn to be patient with others. Everything I do is to be done for Your glory--yet so often I forget.

Please teach us to wait on Your timing and to be content with what comes our way. Amen.

LESSON TEN

A HUMBLE WIFE

Humility is not thinking less of yourself but thinking of yourself less.

C.S. Lewis

HUMILITY. THE HEART OF THE MATTER is serving each other in love, isn't it? So why do we complicate things so much?

> *Do nothing out of selfish ambition or vain conceit. Rather, in humility value others above yourselves, not looking to your own interests but each of you to the interests of the others.*
>
> PHILIPPIANS 2:3-4

The opposite of humility would be egotism, otherwise known as being self-centered. Our society feeds off this mindset. People are driven by a desire for fame, applause, and the admiration of their peers. We want to leave our mark in this world, and the bigger the mark—the better.

I'm reminded of an episode of "Little House on the Prairie." (Yeah, I'm a big Little House fan).

After Charles builds a folding-leaf table, he sets out to have it mass produced. He was willing to give up everything they had worked for to pursue this dream, including their home. Thankfully he runs into some trouble and chooses a better direction.

Near the end of the episode he's sitting back in his chair talking to a friend when he says, "You know why I started all this? All this work? Because I wanted to be remembered. My initials on a piece of furniture–I wanted strangers to remember me. I wasn't even giving my own children a chance to remember me."

I saw that episode in 1982 and it stuck with me to this day. Whenever I'm self-centered and concerned about what *I* want in this life my thoughts go back to that mark on the table. I'm reminded of what's important in this world–*love*.

The greatest line from the episode is when Caroline says, "If it's a legacy you're after Charles, you can't do better than our children."

That speaks volumes to me. We can't do better than to love and serve the people God has put in our lives, can we?

You see, leaving a mark on this world is different than leaving a mark on the heart of another. Whether we love our children, our spouse, a sick parent, or friend… we can't do better than love.

I remember the night I found out that one of the books I co-authored hit the *New York Times* best-sellers list. I was so excited that I could barely dial the phone to share the news. It was an honor.

But does it matter? Does any of this matter? Do I really need to make my mark on this world?

No.

I matter to a God who loved me before I loved Him. One who cared enough to send His son to die for my sins so that I might live. He's all that matters.

There isn't a red carpet, a trophy, or a list that could elevate us to a place any higher than that.

And YOU matter--right where you are; right at this moment. You were created and are loved by an almighty God. That's what really matters in this mixed-up world of fame and fortune.

Purpose is found in those quiet moments when no one but *God* sees the work of your hands.

The day will come when we take our last breath, bow for the last curtain call, and leave this world on our journey to home. And when that day comes self-gratification will be nothing but dust in the wind.

Humility is found in many forms such as modesty, meekness, humbleness, lowliness of mind, and submission. These are all virtues that go against our natural desire to excel and be seen in this world. We are driven by a need to be right, to be in charge and to come first. Time and again, our flesh deceives us into thinking that settling for anything less is a sign of weakness.

Jesus was rejected by His people because He didn't meet their expectations. They wanted a king, who would be triumphant over their enemies, but instead they saw a man who was oppressed and afflicted and brought as a lamb to the slaughter. They wanted strength, but what they found was a weak and broken man who refused to strike back.

It's amazing what people miss out on when they refuse to open their eyes. What they failed to see is the same thing that many people fail to see today, which is the incomparable power of humility.

Humility, submission, and lowliness of mind can only occur when the soul is triumphant over the flesh–when our desire to come first is put aside for the good of another. Or, in the case of our Savior and Lord, His desire was put aside for the good of mankind.

Let's take a look at the following verses:

> *Therefore doth my Father love me, because I lay down my life, that I might take it again. No man taketh it from me, but I lay it down of myself. I have power to lay it down, and I have power to take it again. This commandment have I received of my Father.*
>
> JOHN 10:17-18, KJV

Do you see the power in those two verses? It's incredible! There wasn't a single moment during His life when Jesus was under the thumb of mankind. Every step that He took to the cross was a willful and deliberate act of service to His Father.

In the same way, submission is a willful and deliberate act of service that we bring to the Lord. Our flesh wants nothing more than to be in control, to win every argument, and to put ourselves first. Those who exercise humility take up their cross daily by laying down the desire of the flesh for the good of another.

Did you notice the word I used there? *Exercise.* Just like athletes who are training for a race we must train ourselves to be patient, hold our tongue, give up our need to be right, and choose joy. The stronger we get the more power we have over the flesh.

Then said Jesus unto his disciples, If any man will come after me, let him deny himself, and take up his cross, and follow me.

MATTHEW 16:24, KJV

The next time you're told that submission is a step back for women, remember that every step that you take to the cross is a willful and deliberate act of service to God.

S-O-A-P

Scripture
Read Philippians 2:1-18

Observation
What are some of your personal observations from this lesson?

Application
How can you apply this to your life?

Prayer
Dear Heavenly Father,

Please teach me to love and to serve the people that you have put in my life. Help me to grow in the likeness of Jesus Who came to serve rather than to be served. May I learn to be a wife that lives beyond herself. Help me see the value in the blessing that You have bestowed upon us and our marriage. Amen.

LESSON ELEVEN

A FAITHFUL WIFE

Yet when I surveyed all that my hands had done and what I had toiled to achieve, everything was meaningless, a chasing after the wind; nothing was gained under the sun.

ECCLESIASTES 2:11 (NIV)

HUNT AND PURSUE.

Most of us do it, but why? Remember how Abraham sent out his servant out to find Isaac a wife? Or what about the time when the tribe of Judah chased Adoni-Bezek, and cut off his thumbs and big toes? (Ouch! Graphic story there, but he did have it coming!) And let's not forget Pharaoh chasing the Israelites across the Red Sea.

What about us modern day wives? In which ways do we hunt?

We search for a great pair of shoes, the best deal on a car, the right blend of mocha, a well-paying job, cheap underpants for the boys, and the best price for beef.

And then there are the deeper things we pursue such as the need for intimacy, friendship, and love.

I used to wonder why it seemed that everyone had an addiction of some sort. Everyone had an obsession, a fascination, or a need that inspired the way they played house.

Then I came to the understanding that the hand of our Maker has woven pursuit through each one of our souls in hopes that we might turn that hunger to Him.

> *Love the Lord your God with all your heart and with all your soul and with all your mind and with all your strength.*
>
> MARK 12:30 (NIV)

And we do love Him, but we love the low price of beef more, so we run to the market with meatloaf on our mind, all the while telling ourselves that God doesn't mind waiting—we'll talk to Him later...

And hopefully we do. But too often we don't because we heard that the mall was having a sale, we have a few phone calls to make, and...

Hunger, pursuit, fascination, obsession, and desire–all passions I've replaced with the things of this world, when what I really desired was *Him*.

Yes, I was created to chase, but unless I'm chasing the Lord, I'll always be left feeling empty and void.

> *So do not worry, saying, 'What shall we eat?' or 'What shall we drink?' or 'What shall we wear?' For the pagans run after all these things, and your heavenly Father knows that you need them. But seek first his kingdom and his righteousness, and all these things will be given to you as well.*
>
> MATTHEW 6:31-33, (NIV)

Then there are those wives who say, *I'm serving the Lord, I'm praying, I'm reading my Bible, I'm doing everything I should be doing, but I'm not seeing a change in my marriage.*

I remember the year my neighbor and I both planted daisies.

We were two young wives in love with the idea of having a little flower garden all to ourselves. Maybe the idea came to us over a cup of tea, or perhaps it was something we noticed on one of our many afternoon walks. Regardless of what triggered the idea, it was on both of our minds in the spring of 1994.

Sure, we could have taken the easy road and went straight for the potted plants, but seeing that we were young wives on tight budgets we purchased a few packets of seeds with the little change that we had.

Surely that would do the job, wouldn't it?

After carefully preparing the ground, I sprinkled the seeds according to direction, lightly covered them with soil, watered the ground, and then then stood back to let nature take its course.

Hours turned into days, days turned into weeks, and weeks turned into months… all the while not a single seed gave birth to a daisy. Certainly there was plenty of growth to be excited about, but each and every time it was nothing but another weed.

Thankfully I didn't let that experience discourage me. Instead I continued to plant flowers over the years–some grew better than others.

I'll never understand why some plants refuse to grow and others, like my salvia plants, multiply under my care. I don't really have to do anything special to them; they just keep multiplying and getting healthier year after year.

My lupines? They're a whole other story.

I'm reminded of a scripture found in the book of Ecclesiastes. It's a good one for wives and for moms who are sprinkling seeds among those they love.

> *He that observeth the wind shall not sow; and he that regardeth the clouds shall not reap. As thou knowest not what is the way of the spirit, nor how the bones do grow in the womb of her that is with child: even so thou knowest not the works of God who maketh all. In the morning sow thy seed, and in the evening withhold not thine hand: for thou knowest not whether shall prosper, either this or that, or whether they both shall be alike good.*
>
> ECCLESIASTES 11:4-6 (KJV)

What Solomon is saying here is "Carpe Diem!" Seize the day, ladies! The farmer who sits around waiting for perfect weather conditions misses out on the harvest because the sun, the wind and the rain will always be out of his control.

Nature is in the palm of God's hand. The farmer's job is to get out there and plant the seeds—it's the Lord's job to bring forth the harvest.

All he asks is that we're faithful in well doing.

In other words, if we sit around waiting for a perfect husband or a perfect marriage *before* we plant seeds, we're missing the mark.

If we're discouraged because we're not seeing results, we need only to lean on the Father. Our job is to love our husbands according to the will of God today—right now—and to trust Him with our future.

The heart of our husband is in the palm of God's hand to do with as He will.

Let's Take a Lesson from Ruth

Last summer I took a bus—make that a few. I hadn't taken a city bus in about fifteen years, but I felt it was time for a new adventure.

Can you call going to the passport office downtown an adventure? I think my kids would. And we did.

I was a stranger in a foreign land.

At least it felt foreign to me—not the road I'm used to traveling, nor the means.

The first day I went with my daughter, and I had so many questions, "What's this for? What's that? Why is that seat flipped up...?"

Followed by, "Don't push that, mom!"

It was all very exciting to me. And we even met a few panhandlers while we were at it.

The next day I was called back to the passport office. This time the boys came with us and brought one of their friends.

While we were out and about, Madison picked up a vintage typewriter from one of the antique stores. We're told it's a 1920 model. And if you've ever seen one of these babies, you might have noticed that it's a heavy little piece of equipment.

Just carrying it from the store to the bus took a lot of effort on Madison's part. Thankfully the boys were with us to help carry the load. But here's the thing... it wouldn't have been so bad if I hadn't hopped on the wrong bus—twice. Yeah, I was a little mixed up with bus routes that lead us all over downtown before we were finally on our way home.

You know what I noticed in all of this? *The kids trust me.* It wouldn't have mattered where I took them, or how many twists and turns there were in the road, they were secure in the knowledge that I'd keep them safe wherever they went.

I got to thinking about Ruth, and how she chose to follow her mother-in-law into a strange land. The thing about Ruth is—she was secure in the knowledge that God would keep her safe where ever she went.

> *Ruth replied, "Don't urge me to leave you or to turn back from you. Where you go I will go, and where you stay I will stay. Your people will be my people and your God my God.*
>
> RUTH 1:16

What is particularly interesting about Ruth is that she is the only woman (other than the Proverbs 31 woman) that the Bible refers to as "virtuous." The earliest use of the word referred to men of strength, and is now commonly defined as "moral character."

Ruth was faithful and it showed in her character:

She Surrendered Her Life

The decision that Ruth made to follow Naomi required a complete surrender of all that she had. She was a Moabite who was not only leaving her home, but also leaving her people behind. There was a long history of conflict between the Moabites and the Israelites so choosing to live with them was a giant step of faith and a great sacrifice.

She Worked Hard

Hard work is a virtue. We see it in the virtuous character of Ruth, and again in Proverbs. Ruth went out to the fields daily to glean.

And Ruth the Moabitess said unto Naomi, Let me now go to the field, and glean ears of corn after him in whose sight I shall find grace. And she said unto her, Go, my daughter.

RUTH 2:2

She Was Humble

Ruth new that she was a stranger in the land and didn't take their kindness for granted. In the same way we aren't to take our faith for granted. It is a privilege and honor to be united with God.

Then she fell on her face, and bowed herself to the ground, and said unto him, Why have I found grace in thine eyes, that thou shouldest take knowledge of me, seeing I am a stranger?

RUTH 2:10

Her Kindness Was Evident

Ruth did so much for her mother Naomi that her kindness was evident to all who knew them.

And Boaz answered and said unto her, It hath fully been shewed me, all that thou hast done unto thy mother in law since the death of thine husband: and how thou hast left thy father and thy mother, and the land of thy nativity, and art come unto a people which thou knewest not heretofore.

RUTH 2:11

She Was Faith-Focused

Ruth was mindful of where she came from, and she desired to serve the God of the Israelites—the one true God. She was willing to give up everything that she had to be a part of His people and their faith.

She Prepared Herself for Her Kinsman Redeemer

Ruth was instructed by her mother-in-law to do three things before going to see Boaz. She was to wash herself, anoint herself, and put her "raiment" on. This is an example to all of us that we must prepare ourselves for the return of our Savior.

S-O-A-P

Scripture

Read Ruth 1

Observation

What are some of your personal observations from this lesson?

Application

How can you apply this to your life?

Prayer

Dear Heavenly Father,

I pray that I will grow strong in faith. Help me to trust you along every step of the journey even when I don't know where the path leads. During those moments when we don't sense your presence, help us to exercise faith.

May we grow strong as a couple in a Christ-centered marriage. And may our lives bring glory to You. Amen.

LESSON TWELVE

A FORGIVING WIFE

Forgiveness is the fragrance that the violet sheds
on the heel that has crushed it.

MARK TWAIN

RUTH BELL GRAHAM ONCE SAID, "A happy marriage is the union of two good forgivers."

This gives us a glimpse into one of the strongest marriages of our time. Married over sixty years, Ruth and Billy Graham understood that anger is inevitable–it comes easy–but forgiveness comes with sacrifice.

One of the first fights I ever had with Michael came three years into our marriage. Can you believe that? Three years! I was pregnant with our first child, and my emotions were running wild on me. I remember sitting in the baby's room folding little undershirts while tears streamed down my cheeks. The slam of the apartment door told me he was walking off steam.

I don't even remember what we were fighting about, but I do remember that it hit me straight to the gut. I felt like I had just lost my best friend and that everything we built over the years collapsed in a matter of minutes.

After three years, this didn't feel right to me–this anger thing. Two people in love are supposed to be... well... in love.

I didn't feel that way. All I felt was anger and rejection. My guess is that he felt that way too.

After twenty-five years, I've come to learn that anger is bound to happen. Anger is a natural part of being human. "Losing your cool" on the other hand is giving in to temptation. God instructs us to be self-controlled and forgiving.

> *Be ye angry, and sin not: let not the sun go down upon your wrath:*
>
> EPHESIANS 4:26

This became the number one rule for us from the moment we said I do. We'd always resolve conflict *before* falling asleep. This worked for a while until about seven years into our marriage then Michael fell asleep. That fueled my anger all the more.

How could he fall asleep when we had a covenant to stand by?

What I didn't realize then was that this scripture had little to do with our time zone, and everything to do with calming my spirit so that I could be reconciled to him.

> *Stand in awe, and sin not: commune with your own heart upon your bed, and be still. Selah. Offer the sacrifices of righteousness, and put your trust in the Lord.*
>
> PSALM 4:4-5

"Commune with your own heart." Wow. That spoke to me.

Forgiveness has to start in our own hearts before we can pour it out to another. Anger is natural, but letting it fester is a dangerous thing. It's important to heal fractures in your relationship before they get out of control.

Matthew Henry writes, "Though anger may come into the bosom of a wise man, it rests only in the bosom of fools."

You know that incredible feeling you get after you reconcile with your spouse? Michael and I are affectionate and we're prone to joke around a bit more. The reason we feel that surge of excitement is because reconciliation is something to celebrate.

It reminds us that we're still the same two people in love, and that nothing can come between us as long as we're willing to fight for our marriage, and fight *together* against the world.

It's Not About You

Running a Facebook community of over 160,000 fans means that I'm going to get hundreds of opinions on what marriage should look like. As a result of that I often hear thoughts that stem from a secular view. Thankfully there is a strong community of women out there who are stepping away from the "me" generation to seek God's will for their marriage. But unfortunately there are also those who just don't get why we'd ever want to live to "please our man."

Here's the thing… if your primary goal is to please your husband, you're missing the mark. Our goal is to live according to our created purpose which is that of bringing glory to God.

The world doesn't revolve around us. Everything in it including our lives should revolve around pleasing God.

When we live in harmony with our husbands according to God's plan for our marriage we are pleasing the Lord.

My sister and I clearly remember our school days during the 70's when we were bombarded with the message, "The most important person in the whole wide world is you." In fact this was the title of a song that accompanied many of the videos they played for me and my classmates.

What they weren't teaching us, was to esteem others higher than ourselves.

Thankfully, when we gave our lives to the Lord we understood that life was about more than merely pleasing ourselves, it was about living beyond ourselves so that God would be glorified through our lives.

Marriage must hold the same focus if we're to glorify God.

The union between a man and his wife is a reflection of the covenant between Jesus Christ and the church. Are we presenting that covenant as one that is holy and acceptable unto God? In other words, what is our marriage saying to the world?

And if it calls for forgiveness and grace on our part, are we willing to be that living sacrifice?

We may very well feel that we are perfect just the way that we are, but God's will for our lives is that we are continually growing in virtue.

We don't create a life merely for the benefit of our *husbands*. Although we do love them to pieces and that is a good thing! We live a sacrificial life that is pleasing to *the Lord* and the fruit of that sacrifice is that we are a crown to our husbands.

Fruit is the result, not the goal.

Yes, you have a right to be "happy," but God desires more for you and for your marriage. Temporal happiness doesn't offer the long-lasting joy that one yields through hard work, commitment, and adherence to wisdom.

S-O-A-P

Scripture

Read Ephesians 4

Observation

What are some of your personal observations from this lesson?

Application

How can you apply this to your life?

Prayer

Dear Heavenly Father,

Everything in my life should be centered on You. Yet over and over again, it is centered on me and my wants. It's easy to say that I'm a forgiving person, but when the time comes that I'm called to forgive, I choose to forget the importance of growing in grace.

Help us to heal fractures in our marriage before they get out of control. And grant us the ability to glorify You in all that we do. Amen.

LESSON THIRTEEN

A Joyful Wife

Find out where joy resides and give it a voice far beyond singing. For to miss the joy is to miss all.

ROBERT LOUIS STEVENSON

ASK ANYONE WHO'S BEEN MARRIED FOR over 25 years and they'll tell you that marriage is rewarding, but it's not always easy. Over the years we deal with a number of issues that take their toll on us. Difficult in-laws, financial stress, sick children, renovations, and unemployment are just a few of the things that can drag us down, and often they do.

Two of the biggest problems that young couples face are these:

1) Our expectations are off
2) We're expecting our spouse to make us happy

Our financial expectations were sky high when Michael and I got married. He was earning $7.00/hour and I was earning less. We bought a "handy man's special" assuming that we could fix up the old character home, but once I lost my job, we were barely getting by on his wage alone.

"Don't Pay a Cent" events were appealing to us. I could have a house full of furniture and not pay a cent until 1991. Wow!

We were sold on that until we realized that time flies when you have debts to pay.

This is only one example of how our expectations were off, but over the years we discovered yet more in both our surroundings and our personal flaws.

Through all of it–the good, the bad, and the ugly–there was one important lesson we learned. It's vital and life changing to those who finally get it:

Happiness doesn't come from your spouse–it comes from a Christ-centered life.

Looking to the scriptures, we see verse after verse reminding us that our strength comes from God. Those that wait on Him are refreshed.

Our surroundings can never give us that feeling of joy, peace, and contentment that a life in Jesus Christ can.

> *But they that wait upon the Lord shall renew their strength; they shall mount up with wings as eagles; they shall run, and not be weary; and they shall walk, and not faint.*
>
> ISAIAH 40:31

On his death bed, my father was barely 80 pounds. He was riddled with tumors in his brain and his lungs. Too weak to speak, he pulled Mom in close and gave her a smile that reminded us all how she was the wife of his youth. Over the years, he had learned the important lesson that joy comes from a life that is abandoned to Christ.

As a result, he spent his last days on earth with frail arms raised to heaven. Not a word of complaint.

So how do you get it? How do you move from a life of discontentment and sorrow to one that is spilling over with joy?

Like the song says (and believe me I know because my dad sang it to us 24/7) you turn your eyes upon Jesus, and the things of this world will grow dim.

Day by day, teach yourself to refocus. In EVERYTHING give thanks because in doing so we learn to trust God and see His hand at work in our lives.

During my quiet time, I came across this portion of scripture. I don't know why, but for some reason this spoke to me in a different way than it has in the past.

> *But this I say, He which soweth sparingly shall reap also sparingly; and he which soweth bountifully shall reap also bountifully. Every man according as he purposeth in his heart, so let him give; not grudgingly, or of necessity: for God loveth a cheerful giver. And God is able to make all grace abound toward you; that ye, always having all sufficiency in all things, may abound to every good work:*
> 2 CORINTHIANS 9:6-8

Don't you love it when that happens? When you're reading the Bible and the Spirit moves you stop and consider it deeply? It's incredible.

My dad used to refer to it as scripture jumping off the page. I also think of it as the Word spilling off the page and sinking into my heart.

I realize that Paul is referring to the way that we give here. But today I considered applying it to the way that I live--in particular, the way that I love my husband and parent my children.

It's telling me this: the time and the effort that I put into parenting will come back to me as a reward. When I give of myself *generously* I receive *generously*.

And secondly, dishes are dull, laundry is never ending, and scrubbing a toilet isn't all that much fun. But here's the thing– God loves a cheerful giver. He wants us to experience joy in the journey. He wants us to live and to give from the heart not from the hands.

So how do we do that? How can we experience joy in the midst of the mundane?

Gratitude. It's the antidote for sour grapes. When we're truly grateful for the people, the home, and yes–even the laundry that we have, our attitude takes on the form of gratitude.

Discipline isn't fun. Nor is training. I remember back to the days when I was potty-training my children–it consumed all of my time. I would literally sit beside them and read them a pile of books until a tinkle came out, which in some cases seemed to take all afternoon.

Shopping with four kids was a three-ring circus and I was the clown. One time Nathaniel decided to duck into the men's change room until the staff came looking for him. He was careful not to make a single peep while I was calling out his name at the top of my lungs. But shopping had to be done.

Discipline is tough. It takes time and it takes patience to do it right.

In the same way that self-discipline brings fruit of righteousness to those who are exercised by it, it develops fruit in the vineyard of a growing family.

It wasn't until recent years, that I realized just how important our happiness is to my husband and why.

He delights in the joy of his family because he sees our gratitude as a reflection of *his* gift to *us*.

If we're on vacation and everyone is having a great time, as our provider, he gains a sense of accomplishment. If we're at the beach and the kids are laughing and splashing away in the water I can tell that my husband is exactly where he wants to be. One look at his smile confirms I am right.

Just this past Sunday he spent time taking the roof and doors off of our jeep so that we could enjoy fireworks from the comfort of our car. Then he spent over an hour in heavy traffic trying to find us a great place to park. We had an amazing time watching the fireworks, in fact it was one of the best days I've had in a long time.

On our way home I made sure to tell him what an incredible day that I had, "I haven't enjoyed a day as much as this one in years," I said. "Thank you!" And it couldn't have been any truer. The night sky was beautiful, the kids were in the back seat and we were feeling the wind in our hair.

I could tell by the tone of his response that he was blessed by my encouragement and my appreciation.

I love the sounds of a happy home: music playing sewing machine humming, treadmill tapping, clocks ticking, pages turning, noses sniffling, dishes clattering in a sink of soapy water, the gentle pitter patter of slippered feet… Few things in this life are orchestrated as beautifully as the concerto of family life. And we as mothers hold the power to direct the rhythm it holds.

And if you're not joyful? If you've have a bad day and you've missed out on the joy–what then?

Remember that God's grace is upon you. Yes, He loveth a cheerful giver, but He also loves you during those times when you're down on yourself for doing everything wrong.

S-O-A-P

Scripture

Read Romans 5

Observation

What are some of your personal observations from this lesson?

Application

How can you apply this to your life?

Prayer

Dear Heavenly Father,

You are my rock, my salvation, my strength and my joy. Nothing in this world could ever compare to the riches of your mercy and grace.

Teach me to give from the heart. Not out of duty, but with a gladness that comes from serving You. Amen.

A PASSIONATE WIFE

Be passionate and move forward with gusto every single hour of every single day until you reach your goal.

AVA DUVERNAY

WHEN I WAS DATING MICHAEL, I was on a passionate pursuit for him. In other words, there was an intense chase going on. He didn't always see it because I was good at being subtle. But behind every phone call, every outfit, and every love note I wrote, there was a whole lot of planning going on behind the scenes.

I was crazy about this guy (still am!).

I doodled his name in my notebooks, I sat by the phone waiting for his call, and I had a good dose of the butterflies. Love had me walking through the mall for about six hours because he mentioned that he just might go shopping. I didn't find him that day, but I did manage to pick up a pair of adorable shoes–which I was also passionate about.

After two years, the chase came to a halt when we finally stood at the altar reciting our vows. I was his, he was mine, and there was nothing on this planet that could break us apart.

I didn't have to sit by the phone waiting for his call, and I didn't have to walk through the mall hoping to catch a glimpse of his smile. I was waking up next to him every day, and from what I could see, he wasn't about to go anywhere.

But here's the thing. While my pursuit for this man might be over, the pursuit for his heart is an ongoing passion of mine. Like anyone else, I have a choice to either live a self-centered life or to live one that reflects my walk with the Lord.

We weren't created to live a bland life; we were created to live a passionate one. To come to a full understanding of God's grace and vigorously pursue our Savior.

In the same way, God created marriage to be a union that would reflect the relationship between Jesus Christ and His passionate church.

We were created to bring glory to God through the way that we live and the way that we love. To be servants of grace who give more than we're given and forgive *before* we're forgiven.

He came to give us life in abundance, because He knows that those who are exercised by faith possess the fruit of righteousness that brings peace and joy to our lives.

Marriage is ordained by God, and when we live out our vows according to His incredible wisdom and grace—love never fails.

> *Love is patient, love is kind. It does not envy, it does not boast, it is not proud. It does not dishonor others, it is not self-seeking, it is not easily angered, it keeps no record of wrongs. Love does not delight in evil but rejoices with the truth. It always protects, always trusts, always hopes, always perseveres.*
>
> 1 CORINTHIANS 13:4-6, NIV

It's one thing to *feel* passionate about your spouse and another to *be* passionate about your marriage.

In many cases, the momentary passion is gone from a marriage, so is one spouse or the other. If we simply equate love with emotion we're missing out on the blessings of a God-ordained union.

Marriages often end because people get caught up in the cycle of discontentment. Many marry over and over again thinking *this one will be different.* Linda Wolfe from Indiana holds the record at being married 23 times.

I don't know about you, but I'd rather be married 23 years.

We could walk away when we're bored, but that desire for passion will only come back again and again unless we fill that space with a passionate pursuit for something more than a few butterflies in our tummy and the warmies at night.

Passion is good when our focus is in the right place. If we hunger for a better marriage and strive in our walk with God we can achieve powerful growth. The choice is ours.

God didn't create this incredible union to be tiresome, lifeless, and dull, but that rather through obedience to faith we might experience life in abundance.

People who sit around bored, complaining that life is dull won't be accomplishing much. We have the power to ignite a fire in our marriage and in our walk with the Lord.

One single spark can set a field on fire, one spark can ignite wrath or greatness, and one spark can change the course of your marriage. That's all it takes to get started—one spark.

S-O-A-P

Scripture

Read John 4:1-24

Observation

What are some of your personal observations from this lesson?

Application

How can you apply this to your life?

Prayer

Dear Heavenly Father,

I pray that you will give us a burning desire to fight for our marriage. May we learn the joy that comes with contentment and the peace that comes from doing Your will.

Give us a growing passion to honor in the way that we live and the way that we love. Amen.

LESSON FIFTEEN

A RADIANT WIFE

There are no better cosmetics than a severe temperance and purity, modesty and humility, a gracious temper and calmness of spirit; and there is no true beauty without the signatures of these graces in the very countenance.

ARTHUR HELPS

IT'S NOT EVERY DAY THAT WE wake up the kids at 2 am to go for a drive, but the other night we knew we had to.

There was a meteor shower that night, and we certainly didn't want them to sleep through it. Not with the star-gazers I have! So we put the roof down on the jeep, grabbed a couple of blankets to cover up with, and went for a drive in the country.

Knowing how beautiful the sky can be when it's completely dark, we were determined to get as far away from the city lights as we could without driving all night. Finally, after passing what smelled like a pig barn, a skunk, and a mustard field, we turned onto an old gravel road, parked the car beside a corn field and set our eyes on the sky.

It was breathtaking.

But then again, when isn't the sky a breathtaking sight? From the brilliant color of a clear blue sky to the magnificent sight on a dark stormy night, it's truly amazing to witness the glory of God.

With the roof down, we were able to stand up on our seats or sit on the roll bars to get the best view. I think I saw about twenty shooting stars that night. Most of them were small, but two of them appeared to leave a brilliant trail behind them lasting only a second or two. If you looked away for a second you missed it, which is why we encouraged the kids to keep watch.

Madison was afraid of the corn field that loomed beside us. You don't realize how tall corn is until you're standing next to a mature crop, do you? As least us city folks don't. It must have been about ten feet tall–absolutely beautiful.

On the drive home I got to thinking about the words of the Psalmist:

> *The heavens declare the glory of God; the skies proclaim the work of his hands. Day after day they pour forth speech; night after night they reveal knowledge.*
> PSALM 19:1-2, NIV (EMPHASIS ADDED)

And then I got to thinking about a conversation I had awhile back with someone who asked me what glory was.

I think it's one of those Christian buzz words like "worship" and "holy" that we often use, but perhaps we don't consider the weight of them as deeply as we should.

We are called to glory. And the reason we're called to bear fruit as a Christian is so that our lives would bring glory to God.

> *According as his divine power hath given unto us all things that pertain unto life and godliness, through the knowledge of him that hath called us to glory and virtue.*
> 2 PETER 1:3

My favorite way to describe glory is radiant beauty. When we glorify God His radiant beauty shines through us much like the stars on a clear summer's night.

We can also give glory to God by worshiping Him, but then again the best way that we can worship Him is by loving Him and loving others to Him.

When we live and love the way that Christ did, we reflect the beauty of God's mercy and grace. We are His light in this world, and just like the stars–the darker the world is, the brighter He shines.

I can kneel in prayer all day saying, "Lord, I love you, I love you, I love you…" but if I don't love Him enough to be His hands and His heart in this world, my words are in vain.

Declaring His glory to the lonely and lost is the most breathtaking way we can worship the Lord!

Jesus said, *"I have glorified thee on the earth: I have finished the work which thou gavest me to do."*

Another way of looking at radiance is through nature.

I live up in Manitoba, Canada where spring is deceptive at times. We can have beach weather one day, and as soon as everybody exchanges their warm clothes for flip flops and tank tops, we discover that we're expecting two inches of snow.

I'm cautious when it comes to planting my garden, because I've learned over the years not to trust the warm weather. But I wasn't always this smart–we've had several years where I planted early in the spring and spent countless nights covering my plants with bed sheets and table cloths due to frost warning.

My yard looked silly at times with several bed sheets draped over the plants, and of course I looked ridiculous because I was the only woman on the block that was too anxious to follow the one rule of thumb, "Wait until May Long Weekend to plant."

When it comes to plants, I love the beauty of annuals. The colors and the variety of flowers take my breath away. Once the garden is full, I can hardly resist buying yet a few more, but I've come to discover one thing–their beauty fades quickly. I put the flowers in on May long weekend and they start fading by August.

Each spring I used to invest in more flowers, until I discovered perennials. The beauty of perennials is that their strength lies beneath the face of the earth. It doesn't matter how severe our winters are or how many feet of snow cover the garden--they return each and every year stronger and healthier than they did the year before.

Perennials can withstand frost in the early spring because their root remains untouched. Long-lasting beauty and strength add to their value, much like the radiant heart of a woman who is grounded in Christ.

A woman whose heart takes root in the Lord possesses a radiance that lasts longer than her youth ever will. She is a strong force in the face of tribulation and trials because she knows that her heart is safe in the hands of the Lord. The beauty within her draws the heart of her husband close to her own.

Charm is deceptive, and beauty is fleeting; but a woman who fears the LORD is to be praised.

PROVERBS 31:30, NIV

"More of you, Lord--less of me." Those are the transforming words of a beautiful woman. Words that hold the power to unlocking a treasure that lies beneath the skin of this fading world.

S-O-A-P

Scripture

Read Philippians 2

Observation

What are some of your personal observations from this lesson?

Application

How can you apply this to your life?

Prayer

Dear Heavenly Father,

As I begin this day, guide my mouth in all I say that it would be pleasing to you... that my thoughts would give you praise....that my hands would bless those around me... that my feet would walk in Your paths. Grant me wisdom that I would be pure before you Lord. Amen.

LESSON SIXTEEN

A BALANCED WIFE

Out of clutter, find simplicity. From disorder, find harmony. In the middle of difficulty lies opportunity.

ALBERT EINSTEIN

Has there ever been better direction for time-management than that which comes from, Proverbs chapter 31? I'm reminded of one popular rule in dieting, "Don't waste calories by diving into the bread basket." Here, the same rings true about life:

> *She watches over the affairs of her household and does not eat the bread of idleness.*
>
> PROVERBS 31:27, KJV

My job as a keeper of the home is to watch over the affairs of my household. This means that I need to engage myself in the home, watching over the affairs of each and every person therein. Where are my children? What video games are they playing? What books are they reading? Who are their friends? Is anything troubling my husband?

These are a few of the things we notice when we're actively involved with the family. With one look my husband can tell when something is bothering me, and I can tell in a split-second when Nathaniel is guilty about something. The more face-time (and I'm not talking about iPhones here) I have with these people the more I'll understand their needs and how fulfill them.

The thing is most women are busy. There's no doubt about it, but yet I see some incredible wives who manage their house well, raise God-fearing children, have a great marriage, find time to write books, take classes, run small businesses, or work outside the home.

HBut how is it possible for anyone of us to do it all and still be engaged with the family?

It isn't. There isn't one of us who can do "it all," but we can manage to get a lot done when we put our affairs in order. That's where the second part of that verse comes in when it talks about *eating the bread of idleness.*

Consider the old saying, "There's a place for everything, when everything is in its place." While that's true, I'll also add this, *there is no place for anything when junk is in its place.*

I can't find the space to put my bath towels when my hall closet is packed with sewing supplies that date back as far as 1992. I can't find room for soup ladles in a drawer that's accumulated broken and useless utensils for the past 23 years.

We can visualize this problem when it comes to the drawers and closets in our home because the stuff eventually starts to fall out, but it's a little harder to see when we're talking about the closets and drawers of our life.

What I mean by this is that the storage spaces we refer to as "time" tend to fill up with phone calls, watching television, browsing the internet, hanging out with our friends, sitting out in the sun, oversleeping, and the like.

And then there are cell groups, Sunday school classes, church camp, women's conferences, teaching, leading, speaking, cooking, helping…

Which activities do we choose, and which ones do we step back from?

I'm the kind of person that wants to sign my name on every page. I'd love to be involved, and I wish there were ten of me to go around.

Michael, on the other hand, wisely steps back and says, "Maybe we should think about this, Darlene," because he knows that there aren't ten of me. With four kids, there's barely *one* of me some days.

I get so caught up in the thrill of opportunity that I forget to take my ideas to God. Bad move. After all isn't He the one who knows my agenda better than anyone else?

Now listen, you who say, "Today or tomorrow we will go to this or that city, spend a year there, carry on business and make money." Why, you do not even know what will happen tomorrow. What is your life? You are a mist that appears for a little while and then vanishes. Instead, you ought to say, "If it is the Lord's will, we will live and do this or that."

JAMES 4:13-15, NIV

Looking at that verse, I don't believe that James is *discouraging* us from planning for the future. What he's *encouraging* us to do is to put our will in the hands of God, boast in Him alone, and follow His lead.

But how can we possibly know God's will for our lives if we don't take things to Him in prayer? If we don't read the Word? We won't, unless something stands in our way.

I'm reminded of Balaam in Numbers chapter 22. God clearly instructed Balaam not to go to the Israelites, but after being enticed to do so he sets off on his journey to curse them. When his donkey saw the angel of the Lord standing in their path with a sword drawn in his hand, the donkey turned away and refused to go forward. After being punished by Balaam, the donkey turned another way, but the angel of the Lord stood in his path yet again. Penned in, the donkey threw himself against the wall, crushing Balaam's foot.

Finally, with no way left to turn, the donkey fell down, and the Bible tells us that Balaam's anger was kindled so that he struck the animal with his staff.

That's when God miraculously opened the mouth of the donkey who said, "What have I done unto thee, that thou hast smitten me these three times?"

God was determined to bar Balaam's way.

Have you ever been in situations where you set out to do something and there's a barricade at every turn? This could mean that we need to press on and overcome those obstacles, but there are times when God has no other choice than to protect us from the choices we've made.

The question is, *how do we know if we're following God's will or following our own?*

When faced with important decisions the first question we need to ask is, *Will this be pleasing to God?* In Balaam's situation it was crystal clear that God had instructed him *not* to go. In the same way, when we are making decisions many of the answers might be clearly spelled out in scripture. By developing good Bible study habits we learn those principles and draw from them when we have decisions to make.

A prayer life is important as it leads us to bring our concerns to the Lord and allows Him to speak to our hearts. There will be times when the answer comes to us in a miraculous way such as a word of encouragement from a prayer buddy, but often times God will speak to your conscience, and when He does you'll have a sense of peace about the choice that you make.

You might say to yourself, "Well, of course, teaching Sunday School is God's will–that's a no-brainer!"

But the real question is this, is it God's will for *you?*

Lastly, if your desire is in line with the will of God, but you are still unsure if it's the best thing to do, then dig a little deeper and ask yourself these five questions:

1. If I take this on am I spreading myself too thin?

2. Will this distract me from serving the Lord, or will it encourage my walk?

3. Will it take too much time away from my key priorities such as my husband and my children? Or is it a comfortable fit?

4. What is the purpose of me doing this?

5. Is this decision one that would glorify God?

Be willing to shed some "idle bread" and you'll free up valuable space in your life. Prioritize faith and family first– the rest will fall into place.

S-O-A-P

Scripture
Read Romans 12

Observation
What are some of your personal observations from this lesson?

Application
How can you apply this to your life?

Prayer
Dear Heavenly Father,

Give me confidence to stand up for what I believe in and the strength to carry on your works even when it is hard. When I feel weak, be my strength. When I am unsure, be my wisdom. Guide me and direct my life. My desire is to be a Godly wife and to stand pure before you, Lord. Give me clean hands and a pure heart. Amen.

LESSON SEVENTEEN

A GOOD WIFE

Beautiful people are not always good, but good people are always beautiful.

UNKNOWN

EVER SINCE THE NEW PUPPY ARRIVED I have a never-ending pile of laundry. You wouldn't think a little dog would affect my laundry pile, would you? But she does immensely!

Every time I turn around I see that one of my kids has left a jacket, a towel, or a blanket on the floor which Chelsea views as yet another business opportunity.

In addition to getting after the puppy, I've had to get after the kids, constantly reminding them to pick up after themselves.

The other day I ran upstairs to get changed. She was on my bed less than ten seconds and was already squatting for a tinkle. Another load of laundry was added to the growing pile.

It was during this time that I was gently reminded of this scripture:

And let us not be weary in well doing: for in due season we shall reap, if we faint not. As we have therefore opportunity, let us do good unto all men, especially unto them who are of the household of faith.

GALATIANS 6:9&10

See that part that says, "As we have therefore opportunity, let us do good..."? There's an opportunity waiting for me in the laundry room, there's one at the kitchen sink, and there's another that brings me down to my knees with a scrub brush in hand.

The question is, do I grow weary, or do I see these chores as a way to bless others?

I used to look at work as "work," and there are some days that I still do. I forget the reason I'm doing all of this and lose focus of why I'm here. I grow weary, I get tired, and I get cranky.

Then there are the days when I remember why I'm here. I'm blessed with the privilege of being someone's wife and being a mom. Those are the days when I walk into the laundry room and look at each load as a little gift of love to my family. Those are the days when I remember that a drawer full of clean laundry isn't just a job done, it's a blessing. Those are the days that are good.

Loving your husband... Going out of your way to show him how much...

"This is all well and good, if you're from the 1950s." At least that's what *they* say.

When Michael comes home from work I like to have dinner ready for him. Something he likes. I'll take a few extra minutes to pull my hair up into a bouncy ponytail, and put on one of my prettiest aprons. If I'm so inclined, I might put on a bit of makeup–nothing much, maybe a touch of mascara, a little blush, and some lip gloss.

I tidy up the house and try to have all of my chores done by the time he arrives. It's my way of showing him that I care for our home and I care about us.

Some nights I'll get a little sappy and run my fingers through his hair or cuddle up with him on the recliner--another way of showing him how much I care.

"This is all well and good, if you're from the 1950s." That's what *they* like to say.

The real question however is, *What does the Bible say?*

The aged women likewise, that they be in behaviour as becometh holiness, not false accusers, not given to much wine, teachers of good things; That they may teach the young women to be sober, to love their husbands, to love their children, To be discreet, chaste, keepers at home, good, obedient to their own husbands, that the word of God be not blasphemed.

TITUS 2:3-5

When did loving others and making an effort to please them go out of style?

Earlier this evening my husband and I hosted our Bible study group. By the time our company arrived at 7:00pm the house was clean, the tea was hot, and the brownies were cut into squares.

Little did they know that I had spent the afternoon vacuuming, sweeping and scrubbing the toilet. They also didn't know that I had pulled my hair up into a bouncy ponytail just minutes before they arrived.

Did they need to know? Not really, all that was important to me was that they felt welcome in our home.

We're so used to impressing others in our society. But when it comes to impressing our husbands people are suddenly taken aback.

"Surely she must have June Cleaver Fever."

Romans 12:2 instructs Christians saying, *"Be not conformed to this world: but be ye transformed by the renewing of your mind, that ye may prove what is that good, and acceptable, and perfect, will of God."*

Some people take that to the extreme thinking that we have to dress differently. And yes, we might have to dress differently if our clothing isn't pleasing to God. But the heart of the message is this: we are to dress and to act in a way that conforms to God's will, whether this social system considers it normal or not. We cannot let pop culture dictate the way that we live or the way that we love.

Whether you're from the 50's or living in 2013, God's instructions for marriage are every bit as wise as they always have been. *That's what I like to say.*

S-O-A-P

Scripture
Read Galatians 6

Observation
What are some of your personal observations from this lesson?

Application
How can you apply this to your life?

Prayer
Dear Heavenly Father,

I come before you broken and ready to be used by You, Lord. You know how I have struggled to be a good wife. I have tried to surrender all to you, yet my strength is often waning.

I know that when I am weak YOU are strong. I need You to raise up arms that hang down. I need Your wings so that I might soar. Increase while I decrease. Restore my soul. Amen.

LESSON EIGHTEEN

A COURAGEOUS WIFE

*Courage is the most important of all the virtues, because
without courage you can't practice any other virtue consistently.
You can practice any virtue erratically, but nothing consistently
without courage.*

MAYA ANGELOU

PICKING UP THE PHONE, I HEARD Michael's voice on the other
end, "I got an interesting call," he said. "I just got off the phone
with your doctor."

That was odd since I had just been to their office that
afternoon. Did they forget to tell me something? Did I leave
something behind?

"Uh huh?" I replied. "What did they want?"

"They said that they spoke with you this afternoon, and the
doctor didn't feel like you had a grasp on the situation. They
thought that perhaps you didn't realize the gravity of your
condition."

The heat rose in my face as I listened to his words. Clearly
Michael agreed with the choices I had made, so why couldn't
they?

"Your baby," the doctor said, "if he makes it to term—will likely have Down's Syndrome."

I was okay with that. But by the time I talked to Michael, Spina Bifida had also been discussed as a strong possibility.

"Spina Bifida?" I gasped with one hand over my mouth. I wasn't prepared for that. Life hadn't prepared me for any of this...

Even so, the choices were clear-cut for us. Children are a blessing from God. Period.

And so we refused to entertain the idea of termination. And we refused to undergo any further testing that could potentially harm our child.

This boy was a gift from the Lord and was to be treated as one.

Several months later Graham was born, kicking and screaming his way into this world. Sure he had his fair share of health problems, but nothing compared to what could have been. In fact other than an allergy to nuts every health problem he had is behind us.

Life doesn't prepare us for moments like that, which is why we must prepare ourselves for the journey. Courage is born to those who exercise it through faith.

It starts with seeking God's will for our lives and is exercised through the choices we make.

As parents, we're constantly faced with choices that call us to exercise courage. We started homeschooling when it wasn't so cool to do so. It was the early nineties, which brought one of two responses from people. Either they were absolutely confused by the notion and suggested we were breaking the law, or they assumed we were religious fanatics out of touch with reality.

The words of Reinhold Niebuhr come to mind where they nest in my soul:

God, grant me the serenity to accept the things I cannot change,
The courage to change the things I can,
And wisdom to know the difference.

Courage is the backbone of faith. Without it we can't be a light on a hill that shines through the darkness. With it we step out alone serving unpopular truth in a world that can't grasp who we are.

Back in the day my dad often sang the popular hymn to us, "Tho none go with me still I will follow. No turning back, no turning back..."

And by his example we learned that being different is a natural part of who we are in Christ.

We're not called peculiar people because we wear distinctive clothing or keep our hair a certain way. We're different because we don't conform to pop culture that stands in the way of our faith.

> *But ye are a chosen generation, a royal priesthood, an*
> *holy nation, a peculiar people; that ye should shew forth*
> *the praises of him who hath called you out of darkness*
> *into his marvelous light;*
>
> 1 PETER 2:9

If it hasn't happened already, the day will come when you and your husband have strong choices to make--when your only options are to either stand true to your faith or to give in to opinions around you.

Be strong and of a good courage; be not afraid, neither be thou dismayed: for the Lord thy God is with thee whithersoever thou goest.

JOSHUA 1:9

Stand strong in your faith and get ready to take on the world!

S-O-A-P

Scripture

Read James 1:2-17

Observation

What are some of your personal observations from this lesson?

Application

How can you apply this to your life?

Prayer

Dear Heavenly Father,

I come before Your throne of grace and lay my household at your feet. You see my struggles, You know my heart and I know how awesome You truly are.

Lord I ask that You strengthen me and enable me to be the wife You have called me to be. I know that those who You call You also equip. And so I surrender my weaknesses to You. Please use me. Amen.

ABOUT THE AUTHOR

Darlene Schacht is an ordinary mom, living an extraordinary life, because of who she is through Jesus Christ. As help-meet to her husband Michael, she guides and nurtures their four children, leading them toward a deeper walk of faith.

Her work has been published in anthologies by Thomas Nelson, Tyndale Publishing and Adams Media. As well she has co-authored a book with actress Candace Cameron Bure, the award-winning and *New York Times* Best-Seller, *Reshaping it All: Motivation for Spiritual and Physical Fitness.* You can find Darlene at:

www.timewarpwife.com
www.facebook.com/timewarpwife
www.facebook.com/thegoodwifesguide

If you liked this book, please consider leaving a review at Amazon.